T0375620

LOW CARB
PATRIOTISM

LOW CARB PATRIOTISM

A Diet for America Through History, Facts, Pop-Culture and Heroes

Lisa Malooly

To order additional copies of this book, contact:
Xlibris Corporation
1-888-795-4274
www.Xlibris.com
Orders@Xlibris.com
26357

CONTENTS

This book is dedicated to my parents, Ray and Alice. Thank you for giving me the wings to not only fly, but the love and support to soar.

Thank-you to Susan and Michele, who are my sisters as well as my best-friends. To my brother Alan, one of my heroes from chapter ten. And to Greg, who's more a brother to me than brother-in-law.

Finally, to my nieces and nephews: Ryan, Skyler, Zachary, Cassidy and Hayley.

May you grow-up being the best Americans you can be—

I love you all.

In memory of my grandparents:

Ancil and Mary Royer. Small-town values passed on from generation to generation, with love.

Esau and Afifi Malooly. Immigrants who not only lived the 'American Dream', but shared it with us.

BIOGRAPHY

Lisa Malooly is a third-generation Texan. She is a graduate from both Texas Christian University and the Academy of Radio and Television Broadcasting and has studied abroad in Australia, New Zealand, Fiji, England, France and Italy. An avid traveler, Lisa has also toured Brazil, Ireland, Denmark, Sweden, Finland, Germany and Russia.

As an ESL Instructor at the University of Texas at El Paso and El Paso Community College, Lisa was introduced to students from all over the world. Discussions over history, facts and pop-culture of the United States resulted in *Low-Carb Patriotism*, an introspective, yet entertaining look at the United States of America. Her goal-to spark a newfound interest and 'love of country' amongst a nation divided.

At Lisa's request, 10% of her royalties from this book will go to the American Cancer Society.

Low-Carb Patriotism

America needs a diet—a diet rich in
twenty-first century patriotism.
Low Carb Patriotism offers a light and breezy examination
of America through a regimen of history,
facts, pop-culture and heroes.
Let's get America back in shape . . . and
shape the heroes for America's future

Low-Carb Patriotism

Patriotism is your conviction that this country is
superior to all other countries because
you were born in it.

George Bernard Shaw (1856-1950)[1]

Low-Carb Patriotism

America needs a *diet* . . . a diet rich in Twenty-First Century Patriotism. Cut the *fat* off apathy and start *supplementing* some allegiance and appreciation back into our American *regimen*. The *health* and *well-being* of our country is at risk. It's time to *digest* the State of the Union and *devour* a renewed camaraderie and common-sense amongst our people. *Grasp* the history of our country— there is *strength* in knowledge. Stretch our minds as to the state of patriotism in this country. Let's *exercise* our pride and *return* optimism and vigor into the nationalism of our people. Let's get American patriotism *back in shape*!

10 CHAPTER
EXERCISE PLAN

W̲arm-Up Exercise—Open your mind while reading the light humor and editorial style messages. Don't forget to form your own opinions too!

Strength Training—The power of this exercise is in reacquainting yourself with our country's unique facts, traditions, pop-culture and history. The difficult part of this exercise will be to envision the sacrifices our forefathers made on our behalf and muscle the unique patriotic spirit that shaped our country.

Cool-Down—Take a deep breath and enjoy this liberating and immensely powerful, blissful feeling . . . it's called freedom.

CHAPTER 1

I PLEDGE ALLEGIANCE

*"When I was born, I was so surprised I didn't talk for a
year and a half."*

—Gracie Allen (1906-1954)[1]

DO YOU HAVE A DAWNZERLY LIGHT?

When I was a child, I thought the phrase in the *Star-
Spangled Banner* went like this. *Oh say can you see By the
dawnzerly light.* I always wondered. What is a dawnzerly
light? Where do you buy it and why do you need it?

Another part of the song was confusing to me. *O'er the
ramparts we watched, were so gallantly streaming* Ramparts?
What in the world are ramparts? Do I have to watch them
to be a good American or do I have to watch them because
they were so gallantly streaming?

Where did my education go wrong in that I never
dissected the *The Star-Spangled Banner*? Sure, we memorized
things like the first paragraph of the Constitution and the
Presidents of the United States. But, did you ever have to
write a paper in school on "What Being An American Means
To Me"? Could you write it today as an adult? Could you
write it today without using the word freedom?

Here I am, an unenlightened, ungrateful, grown-up
American who has no use for memorization of all U.S.
Presidents in chronological order except maybe a guest

appearance on *Jeopardy* or being a phone-a-friend—on *Who Wants To Be A Millionaire.*

Aside from my patriotic duty of exchanging as many former U.S. presidents around as fast as I can, (a.k.a. shopping) all in all, I would say I'm a pretty poor patriot.

DO YOU HAVE *"THAT LOOK"*?

The Pledge of Allegiance was said every morning in my elementary school. The words meant nothing to me, something we *had* to say. I didn't understand why adults around me would recite it with such gusto. At public events, adults proudly put their hand over their heart and men were quick to take off their hats. Everyone just had *"That Look".* I couldn't explain *"That Look",* just a faraway look that my elders had in their eyes when they recited the Pledge of Allegiance. I dismissed *"That Look"* and found it insignificant, for I was a little girl more interested in Barbie's and my Easy Bake Oven!

"That Look" was not something I was ashamed of, just something associated with my elders. I put *"That Look"* right up there with all those things in life we say or do as we grow older. Old people phrases such as "Boy we sure need that rain" or "Look how fresh those turnips are!" You know, *older* people stuff. *"That Look"* was something only adults seemed to do.

Decades passed and I had forgotten all about *"That Look".* Then, one night, while reciting the Pledge of Allegiance at a public function after September 11th, I suddenly stopped during the phrase . . . *of the United States of America.* I was overcome with emotion as tears filled my eyes. There I stood, a grown woman, realizing I finally had *"That Look"* . . . that same look I had seen in the face of my elders so many years ago.

I felt ashamed. I spent my entire life taking my freedom for granted. Freedom is a privilege, not a right. As a child, I assumed it was a right. All talk about "war" seemed like something of a myth, a legend of our country so long ago.

My aunt shared many stories about the love letters my uncle wrote to her in World War II.

Here, as a grown woman with *"That Look"* I am faced with much more than the thought of writing a love letter to a soldier. I am faced with the harsh realization that the liberty I enjoyed as a *right,* is actually a *privilege* and one that must constantly be defended.

Our entire country must have *"That Look"*, the appreciation of being a free nation. Pausing to mourn a soldier we never knew, but was probably a pen pal to an ancestor of ours.

We need *"That Look"* when we encounter someone in the military, someone who thinks my country and me are important enough to die for. *"That Look"* is a visible part of being a patriotic citizen of this country and showing pride in being a part of this nation. If we don't have *"That Look"*, then we really do not deserve to be Americans.

* * *

"Man is the Only Animal that Blushes. Or needs to."

—*Mark Twain (1835-1910)*[2]

IS NIXON ONE OF SANTA'S REINDEER?

"I am voting for Ronald Reagan". My father was amused at my declaration, because I was only thirteen years old. But, since "Alex Keaton" on the television series *Family Ties* was a Republican, well I was too! Looking back I feel so ridiculous. I did not know one thing about the Republican or Democratic Party. I let a television show mold my views on politics. Think that is a ridiculous story? Well guess what. It's still happening.

I teach English As A Second Language at a community college. Although, my students are from all over the world, the majority of them are from Mexico. I remember during the 1996 Presidential Election as I listened to the naturalized students who were registered to vote. I eavesdropped on their political thoughts, for talking politics as an instructor was against school policy. In the class, I could only observe.

What I observed surprised me. Most of the students were newly naturalized citizens, eligible to vote without a clear understanding of the political parties and platforms of the United States. I found myself wondering why my students from Mexico were forming direct correlations between political parties in Mexico and the United States. They connected the political parties in Mexico, PRI and PAN to the Republican and Democratic parties of the United States, respectively.

Assuming that the Republican Party is the equivalent of the PRI and is "is the party of the rich", they were decisively against Republicans. I couldn't help but smile to myself, considering some of the "richest" families in America, the Kennedy's, Kerry's and Rockefeller's are Democrats.

My students in that class were a united Democratic front. I was upset that my fellow naturalized citizens were judgmental. Yes me, the same girl who was a devoted Reaganite because of the fictional character Alex Keaton. As Americans, we cannot generalize politics or political parties. We will never grow as a nation as long as we Straight Ticket Vote or have uninformed voters going to the polls. We need to educate newly naturalized citizens, not brainwash them.

It was ridiculous when Bill Clinton granted amnesty to so many illegal aliens, coincidentally before the 1996 Election. It was a cheap shot for extra votes and it is not fair to legal aliens who go through the naturalization process legitimately. I am equally disappointed in Bush's Immigration Law; allowing over eight million illegal immigrants legal status as temporary workers. I am mad at my political leaders for letting things like that slide by. We deserve more from you and you let us down.

"Laws are like sausages. It's better not to see them
being made."

Otto von Bismarck (1815-1898) [3]

HOW POLITICIANS SEE POLITICIANS

"Politicians are the same all over. They promise to build a
bridge even where there is no river."

—Nikita Khrushchev (1894-1971) [4]

"Politics is not a bad profession. If you succeed there are
many rewards, if you disgrace yourself you can always write
a book."

—Ronald Reagan (1911-2004) [5]

"Politics is supposed to be the second oldest profession. I
have come to realize that it bears a very close resemblance
to the first."

—Ronald Reagan (1911-2004) [6]

"I have always felt that a politician is to be judged by the
animosities he excites among his opponents."

—Sir Winston Churchill [7]

TWO GEORGE W'S

George W. #1

George Washington. Mr. One-Dollar Bill himself. As a
child, I'm sure no one dreamed he was destined for politics.
Look, he knocked down the infamous cherry tree and told
his father "I cannot tell a lie". He cannot tell a lie? . . .

probably, the only politician in America to utter those words!
Wooden teeth and all, he ended up doing pretty well for
himself . . . nations' capital is named after him, face eternally
memorialized on Mount Rushmore and he's got one
heckuva monument! It is suffice to say George Washington
was the first to personify the "American Dream". But, notice
his Inaugural Speech is quite humble and almost a touch
apprehensive, as though ole' George knew exactly the
difficult road he was about to pave for generations to come.

George Washington
Excerpts from the First Inaugural Address [8]
In the City of New York
Thursday, April 30, 1789

*Fellow-Citizens of the Senate and of the House of
Representatives: AMONG the vicissitudes incident to life no
event could have filled me with greater anxieties than that of
which the notification was transmitted by your order . . . On
the one hand, I was summoned by my country, whose voice I
can never hear but with veneration and love, from a retreat
which I had chosen with the fondest predilection, and, in my
flattering hopes, with an immutable decision, as the asylum of
my declining years . . . On the other hand, the magnitude and
difficulty of the trust to which the voice of my country called
me, being sufficient to awaken in the wisest and most experienced
of her citizens a distrustful scrutiny into his qualifications . . .
You will join with me, I trust, in thinking that there are none
under the influence of which the proceedings of a new and free
government can more auspiciously commence.*

Way to go Georgie! What an orator! That Inaugural
Address was fantastic! Glorious! Inspiring! Patriotic!

p.s. Does anyone know what the heck he was saying?

I know one thing. If a modern day President used the
word "anxieties" in his opening paragraph, I'd be on the

next slow boat to China! However, as the "Father of Our Country", George Washington was apprehensive and almost prophetic, as though he knew the difficult road upon which our country was about to embark.

GEORGE W. #2

George W. Bush
Excerpt from Inaugural Address[9]
In the city of Washington D.C.
Saturday, January 20, 2001

. . . *The peaceful transfer of authority is rare in history, yet common in our country. With a simple oath, we affirm old traditions and make new beginnings . . . I am honored and humbled to stand here, where so many of America's leaders have come before me, and so many will follow. We have a place, all of us, in a long story—a story we continue, but whose end we will not see. It is the story of a new world that became a friend and liberator of the old, a story of a slave-holding society that became a servant of freedom, the story of a power that went into the world to protect but not possess, to defend but not to conquer. It is the American story—a story of flawed and fallible people, united across the generations by grand and enduring ideals.*

. . . *After the Declaration of Independence was signed, Virginia statesman John Page wrote to Thomas Jefferson: "We know the race is not to the swift nor the battle to the strong. Do you not think an angel rides in the whirlwind and directs this storm?" Much time has passed since Jefferson arrived for his inauguration . . . But the themes of this day he would know: our nation's grand story of courage and its simple dream of dignity. We are not this story's author, who fills time and eternity with his purpose. Yet his purpose is achieved in our duty, and our duty is fulfilled in service to one another. Never tiring, never yielding, never finishing, we renew that purpose today, to make our country more just and generous, to affirm the dignity of our lives and every life. This work continues. This story goes on. And an angel still rides in the whirlwind and directs this storm. God bless you all, and God bless America.*

In comparing these two inaugural speeches, the apprehensive manner of George Washington differs greatly from that of the confident tone of George Bush. George Bush's inaugural speech reflected upon the past, contemplated the present and inspired hope for the future. These inaugural speeches cast a glimpse into the state of our country as we walk through the chronological stages of democracy.

* * *

"In America any boy may become President and I suppose it's just one of the risks he takes."

—*Adlai E. Stevenson Jr. at a speech in Indianapolis September 26, 1952*[10]

* * *

Without trying to sound too much like that annoying old aunt you see once every ten years. You know the one. She walks up to your face, pinches your cheeks and shouts, "Look how much you've grown!" But, indeed, look how much the United States has grown!

It sure seems the confidence of the nation has improved, but it is important to remember, the United States is *still* to this day a relatively young nation in comparison to the rest of the world.

Toast:

(lift glass) "To another 228 years!" "Here! Here!" (gulp)

TEST YOUR KNOWLEDGE OF AMERICAN FACTS:

A Motto of the United States?

1. *Money Talks, The Rest Walks*
2. *In God We Trust*
3. *Looking Good And Feeling It Is The Best Revenge There Is*
4. *At Least Our Country Is Kind Of Fun To Draw!*

The Capital of the United States?

1. Capital U and S
2. Washington, D.C.
3. Crawford, Texas
4. Anywhere Sam Donaldson happens to be reporting

The National Anthem?

1. *Row Row Row Your Illegal Boat, Gently Past INS*
2. *The Star Spangled Banner*
3. *Flip My Burger Uncle Sam, Before I Leave The McDonald's Of Life*
4. *America . . . Where We Have 50 Choices For Miss America And Only 2 For President!*

The National Bird?

1. KFC
2. Bald Eagle
3. Lady Bird Johnson
4. Larry Bird

The National Flower?

1. Daisy Fuentes
2. Rose

3. Well-groomed weeds
4. Do we even have a national flower?

Answers:

All answers are #2. Piece of cake, I know, but . . . now, take a look at the facts below. How much of this did you know?

FACTS THAT . . . MAYBE YOU KNOW, MAYBE YOU DON'T

In God We Trust—As religious sentiment during the Civil War grew, Secretary of the Treasury Salmon P. Chase was inundated with letters urging him to recognize God on U.S. currency. Chase instructed James Pollock, Director of the Mint in Philadelphia, to prepare a motto. IN GOD WE TRUST first appeared on the 1864 two-cent piece and finally circulated on paper currency on October 1, 1957.[11]

Washington District of Columbia—Washington D.C. is named after both George Washington and explorer Christopher Columbus. The motto of Washington D.C. is *Justitia Omnibus* which means 'Justice For All'. Did you notice, George Washington gave his Inaugural Address in New York? New York and Philadelphia were both the nations' capital at one time. Washington D.C. did not officially become the nations' capital until 1800.[12]

Washington D.C. is also the United States' first planned city, designed by Pierre Charles L'Enfant and laid out by Andrew Ellicott. Pierre Charles L'Enfant intentionally imposed a perfect cross upon the landscape. The White House to the north, Jefferson Memorial to the south, the Capitol to the east and the Lincoln Memorial to the west.[13]

The Bald Eagle—Adopted on June 20, 1782. The 'bald' in Bald Eagle comes from the word *piebald*, which means 'marked with white', not because it has a bald head. Our founding fathers and members of Congress disputed for years before deciding on the Bald Eagle as the national bird. It was chosen, for it symbolized strength, courage, freedom and immortality.

Benjamin Franklin was against the Bald Eagle. He felt it would present a voracious and attacking image of our country. He was in favor of the turkey, a more gentile bird.[14]

Can you imagine if the turkey were chosen? We'd be eating our national bird every Thanksgiving! Yuck.

The Rose—Adopted on October 7, 1986. During a formal ceremony in the Rose Garden at the White House on November 20, 1986, President Reagan issued Proclamation 5574: The National Floral Emblem of the United States of America: The Rose.[15]

FINAL QUESTION:

"I'll take *STUPIDLY RUN COUNTRIES for $200 Alex"*

When you read the following five characteristics, which country first comes to mind?

- Obsessive fixation with sports
- Higher and higher taxes
- Demoralizing of the family unit, including the increase in divorce and the breaking apart of family as an entity
- Building enormous armed forces and military bases
- Decay of religion; conviction and the sanctity of religion

A. France
B. United States
C. England
D. None of the Above

Does it sound like the United States to you? Whew! Thank goodness it's not. These characteristics are generalized reasons for the fall of the Roman Empire, according to historian Edward Gibbons as summarized by www.theexaminer.org.[16]

The answer is D.

Ouch. It sure hurts how similar those traits are to the United States.

WHEN IN ROME

Alexander Tyler was a Scottish history and economics professor at The University of Edinburgh. In 1787, he analyzed the "Fall of the Athenian Republic" and wrote the following commentary:

> "A democracy is always temporary in nature; it
> simply cannot exist as a permanent form of
> government. A democracy will continue to exist up
> until the time that voters discover that they can vote
> themselves generous gifts from the public treasury.
> Form that moment on, the majority always votes for
> the candidates who promise the most benefits from the
> public treasury, with the result that every democracy
> will finally collapse due to loose fiscal policy."

Keep in mind, this thesis was written a little over ten years after the 13 Colonies of the United States established their Constitution. He continued,

> "The average age of the world's greatest civilizations
> from the beginning of history, has been about 200

years. During those 200 years, these nations always
progressed through the following sequence:

From bondage to spiritual faith;
From spiritual faith to great courage;
From great courage to liberty;
From liberty to abundance;
From abundance to complacency;
From complacency to apathy;
From apathy to dependence;
From dependence back to bondage."

I don't know what's more frightening. That our country shares the same characteristics as the 'Fall of the Roman Empire' or that we 'fall' somewhere between *from complacency to apathy* and *from apathy to dependence* in Tyler's sequence.

Where do *you* think America stands today?

*   *   *

"Study the past if you would define the future."

—*Confucius*[17]

CHAPTER 2

TO THE FLAG

It seems as though *The Pledge of Allegiance* has been around forever. But in its' original version, the *Pledge of Allegiance* actually received official recognition by Congress in an Act approved on June 22, 1942.[1] That's only a little over sixty years ago!

Have you ever wondered why schoolchildren say *The Pledge* every morning? It was first recited in public schools to celebrate Columbus Day in 1892. The tradition continued and that is why it is said in public schools today.

Originally, *The Pledge* said "*my* flag of the United States of America" instead of "*the* flag of the United States of America". The National Flag Conference in 1923 changed it to *the* flag because they were concerned about the possibility of confusion among foreign-born children and adults who might have the flag of their native land in mind while reciting the Pledge.[2] It may seem trivial changing *my* to *the*, but keep in mind, we were a relatively new nation. We were by 1942 the "Melting Pot" history refers to our nation today.

SUPERBOWL HALF-TIME SHOW 2004

Thanks to the Janet Jackson and Justin Timberlake uh . . . performance . . . the fact that Kid Rock wore an American flag was overlooked. It was a big flag etiquette no-no but most everyone swept it under the rug, probably because

Kid Rock did such a darn good job performing and he wasn't such a boob (no pun intended). His patriotic enthusiasm was magnificent. His performance was endearing and I was a bit jealous that he had that venue to show his love of country with such gusto. But, the costume designer at Superbowl 2004 messed up big-time. First, by not putting enough material on Janet Jackson. Second, by putting the wrong material on Kid Rock. Fashion Police to the rescue? Not this time. It's more like Etiquette Police. But, for reminders, here's a few "rules" for our precious flag.

FLAG ETIQUETTE DO'S[3]

1. Display the flag every day, unless weather conditions can damage it.
2. Display the flag from sunrise to sunset.
3. The flag may be displayed at night, but it must be well-lighted.
4. Always allow the flag to hang free.
5. Hoist the flag briskly when raising it.
6. Lower the flag slowly, gathering and folding it before it touches the ground.
7. Stand at attention facing the flag when it is raised or lowered, passes by in a color guard and during the national anthem.
8. Salute the flag as it passes when wearing a uniform or place your right hand over your heart.
9. Fold the flag properly with a military fold when not in use

FLAG ETIQUETTE DON'T'S[4]

1. Never use the flag for advertising purposes of any manner.
2. Never mark on or attach anything to the flag.
3. Never use the flag as bedding, drapery, or wearing apparel.

4. Never affix the flag to items that will be discarded.
5. Never burn the flag, except to properly discard one that can no longer be used.

FUN FLAG FACTS:

"The Stars and Stripes", "Old Glory", our flag has more nicknames than Jennifer Lopez has engagement rings! Red, white and blue . . . ever wonder why Betsy Ross sewed those colors? And, why stars and stripes? Why not polkadots or a chic animal print?

Here's a few things to know as you encounter the most precious piece of material waving throughout our country today.

The Colors

Red was selected for hardiness and courage
White for purity and innocence
Blue for vigilance, perseverance and justice

Did You Know?[5]

Libya was the first foreign land over which the American flag flew.

The United States flag was placed on the moon on July 20, 1969.

A vexillologist is an expert in the history of flags.

A flag may be held upside down only in the case of extreme emergency. It means "Help Me, I am in trouble!"

William Driver, a naval captain from Salem, Massachusetts, gave the name 'Old Glory' to the flag in 1824.

Records indicate that Francis Hopkinson sent a bill to the Board of Admiralty for his work in designing the flag of the United States.

FLAG FACELIFTS

Plastic surgery, here I come! Liposuction, absolutely. But, I don't think we humans will have nearly the amount of changes our flag has undergone over the past two-hundred years. In fact, it has changed over 26 times in our history! Here are some highlights.[6]

SURGERY #1—The first flag of the United States was used during the Revolutionary War around 1775. It was called the Continental Colors and represented the 13 Colonies.

SURGERY #2—On June 14, 1777 following the signing of the Declaration of United States, the Continental Congress ordered the creation of the first official flag. It contained 13 alternating red and white stripes with 13 white stars against a blue background.

Two new states joined the Union 1794, and five more by 1817.

SURGERY #3—On April 1818, Congress approved using 13 stripes again and each time a new state joined the Union, their star would appear on the flag on the July 4th following their date of entry.

SURGERY #4—The flag's 48 stars were on the flag in 1912.

SURGERY #5—In 1959, the 49th star was added when Alaska joined the United States.

SURGERY #6—In 1960, the 50th star was added when Hawaii joined the United States.

WHO'S ELIZABETH GRISCOM?[7]

Elizabeth was a fourth generation American. Born on January 1, 1752, her ancestry traces back to a line of Quaker's who immigrated from England. When she finished school, her father apprenticed her to a local upholsterer. Today we think of "upholsterers" as sofa-makers or even furnishers, but in colonial times they performed every kind of sewing job, including flag-making. At her job, Betsy fell in love with another apprentice, John Ross, who was the son of an Episcopal assistant rector at Christ Church. A Quaker and an Episcopal! Unthinkable! An inter-denominational marriages was a serious social thumbs—down in the Quaker world, the punishment was to isolate emotionally and economically from the Quaker society. The young 21-year-old Elizabeth Griscom ran away and eloped with John Ross. Now do you know her? She is the famous Betsy Ross!

*FYI: Their wedding certificate was signed by New Jersey's Governor, William Franklin, Benjamin Franklin's son. Three years later William had a permanent rift with his father because he was against the cause of the Revolution.[8]

John and Betsy Ross started their own upholstery business in Philadelphia, tough considering she had been banished from Quaker circles and competition was incredibly fierce. Lucky for Betsy, her new religion would allow her to sit some Sunday's next to America's new Commander-In-Chief, George Washington. Rubbing elbows with the soon-to-be "Father of our Country", not bad. But, the war with Britain was stirring a strong patriotic split, many still felt themselves citizens of Britain, while others were revolutionaries longing for independence.

Betsy and John Ross' upholstery business suffered as a result of the war. Fabrics were hard to come by and business was just plain slow. John joined the Pennsylvania militia and was severely wounded in an explosion and died.

In 1776, Betsy had that fateful meeting with George Washington, George Ross, and Robert Morris. During this meeting they commissioned her to sew the first flag. A widow now, Betsy was allowed to return to the Quakers, who were supporting the war effort. She married again in June of 1777, to a sea captain named Joseph Ashburn. On a trip to the West Indies to obtain war supplies for the Revolutionary cause, Captain Ashburn was captured by the British and sent to Old Mill Prison in England where he died in March 1782.

Third Time's A Charm

Betsy learned of her husband's death from an old friend, John Claypoole, who was also imprisoned at the Old Mill Prison. In May of 1783, Betsy took her third trip down the aisle with, guess who . . . yep, John Claypoole. The couple had five daughters: Clarissa Sidney, Susannah, Rachel, Jane, and Harriet. Her husband initially worked in her upholstery business and then at the U.S. Customs House in Philadelphia, but finally died in 1817 after a long illness. Betsy never remarried, yet continued working and brought many of her immediate family into the business with her. Betsy died on January 30, 1836 at the age of eighty-four. Betsy Ross probably never dreamed that from her fateful meeting with George Washington, her name would go down in history as the person who sewed the first American flag.[9]

WHY THE SONG SAYS " . . . that our flag was still there"[10]

—Star-Spangled Banner

Around 1812, Georgetown was a booming little town of about 5,000 people. Patriotism energized this city, for the Capital and the White House were just a few miles away. A young lawyer named Francis Scott Key lived there with his wife Mary and their small children. Remember the famous

"Boston Tea Party" of 1773 where America protested Britain's attempts to tax and regulate American goods and shipping? At that time Britain was at war with France and needed money fast. It was only a matter of time before the British invaded America again, this time, in 1812. The British invaded through the Chesapeake Bay area on August 19th, 1814 and five days later, they set fire to the White House, Capitol, and several prominent buildings. By then, President James Madison fled to a safe location. (not to be confused with Vice-President Cheney's 'safe undisclosed location') and the British troops docked in and around the Chesapeake Bay area.

Townspeople came to Francis Scott Key and informed him that the British had taken Dr. William Beanes, a popular town physician, as a prisoner of war. He was being held hostage on the British flagship TONNANT and rumors were flying that Dr. Beanes was going to be hanged. Being that he was an influential lawyer, the townspeople asked Francis Scott Key for his help.

Francis Scott Key and Col. John Skinner, an American negotiator for prisoner exchange, boarded the British ship TONNANT. The British would not release prisoners right away, for they were in the midst of planning the upcoming attack on Baltimore. Key and Skinner were forced to wait out the battle.

The Flag That Started It All

Meanwhile, over at Fort McHenry, the commander, Maj. George Armistead, requested a flag so enormous, the British would be able to see it for miles and miles. Two officers were sent to the Baltimore home of Mary Young Pickersgill, a seamstress, and commissioned the flag. Mary and her thirteen year old daughter Caroline, used 400 yards of high quality wool. The fifteen state stars measured two feet from point to point.Eight red and seven white stripes were cut, each measuring two feet wide. It measured 30 by 42 feet and cost around $405.90 to make.[11]

On the morning of September 13, 1814, at 7 o'clock a.m., the British attacked Major Armistead's army. Key and Skinner were still being held by the British and were forced to wait in the darkness for the battle to end. They waited in the darkness, left wondering who won the battle. When daylight came at last, Gen. Armistead's huge flag was blowing in the breeze and Key thought to himself, America won the battle for **the flag was still there!**

Key, so inspired by the awesome sight of the enormous flag, began to write an impromptu poem expressing his emotion. He scribbled nine more lines on some paper he happened to have on the back of his pocket. Although Key wrote various versions, his brother-in-law, Judge J. H. Nicholson, took one of the versions to a printer and copies were circulated around Baltimore. *The Baltimore Patriot* newspaper printed it for the first time on September 20, 1814.[12] Soon after, the poem spread throughout papers across the country.

Where Are They Now?

And the copies of the original *Star-Spangled Banner*? The version that Key wrote in his hotel September 14,1814, remained in the Nicholson family (his brother-in-law's family) for 93 years. In 1907, the copy was sold to Henry Walters of Baltimore. It was later bought at auction in New York from the Walters estate by the Walters Art Gallery in Baltimore for $26,400. In 1953, The Walters Gallery sold the manuscript to the Maryland Historical Society also for $26,400. The other copy is housed in the Library of Congress.[13]

Moral to this story: Keep your scratch paper. It could be worth thousands of dollars someday!

Today, the *Star-Spangled Banner* begins every sporting event and almost every public gathering in this country, but the first public singing performance of the *Star-Spangled Banner* was by a Baltimore actor. From there, the song took on a life of its' own and remained one of the most popular patriotic songs for over one-hundred years before it was finally adopted as our national anthem on March 3, 1931.[14]

And That Famous Flag?

So what ever happened to that famous Fort McHenry flag that awe inspired Francis Scott Key to scribble . . . *that our flag was still there?* You know, the one that cost a astronomical (back then) $405.90 to make? The flag, our beloved Star-Spangled Banner, went on view for the first time on January 1st,1876 at the Old State House in Philadelphia for the nations' Centennial celebration. Today, it is housed in the Smithsonian Institution's Museum of American History. An opaque curtain protects the tattered flag from light and dust, and because of its fragile condition, is exposed only for a few moments once every hour during museum hours. [15]

> "Some people make headlines
> while others make history."
>
> —*Philip Elmer-DeWitt*[16]

GRAND 'OLE FLAG

Hooray for Jerri Kiley. He is a Vietnam Veteran. He obeyed his Commander-In-Chief and risked his life for people he doesn't even know . . . you and me. He is also the man who held a flag up to Toni Smith, the Manhattanville College Senior Basketball Player who made news by turning her body disrespectfully away from the flag before a game.

Can you believe a fellow American actually turned her head away from our flag, the symbol of our country? She was doing it to protest President Bush's foreign policy. Fine. I can hear it now "but her right to Free Speech" blah, blah, blah . . . But, think for a moment. Can you imagine how ridiculous it would look if every citizen turned their bodies away from the flag every time they disagreed with a politician? We would be a country of fools. No more public *Pledges of Allegiance*, only faceless disrespect.

The 1ˢᵗ Amendment "Right To Free Speech" was not designed to weaken us.

> We will weaken as a country.
> We cannot allow this.

In fairness, Toni Smith is not to blame. It is the educational system that did not teach her the history of America that brought us to freedom, is to blame. Yes, the same educational system that forgot to make me write the paper on "What Being An American Means To Me". Freedom allows her to use her college degree, write letters to politicians or perhaps even run for office herself someday. Instead, our media gave her some cheap press. But, to disrespect the flag, the very symbol of our way of life, one does not deserve the right to enjoy the country whose symbol is disrespected.

To get a little insight on our educational system, this is a quote from her stat page from Manhattanville College. Toni Smith quote: "If you don't stand for something, you will fall for anything. It will be a great day when our schools get all the money they need and the military has to hold a bake sale to buy a bomber." [17]

. . . *and the military has to hold a bake sale to buy a bomber?* Who was her Military History professor? Since when are "bombers" and "the military" our enemies? The "military", to which she so disrespectfully refers, allows her the freedom to get an education, play basketball, and live a free and wonderful life. If she were an oppressed woman in Afghanistan, I bet she would beg for a "military" and some "bombers".

As for the schools getting all the money they need, President Bush allocated money for our educational systems. It's the States' poor distribution of the money that seems to be the problem.

I remember the horror of September 11th but, I also remember the comfort that those "bombers" and "military" were protecting me from further harm.

No American should be disrespectful toward the flag.

*   *   *

Imagine this horrible scenario—What if the entire United States Military stopped and said, "You know what? I'm sick of putting my life on the line for a bunch of ungrateful civilians" and walked out on protecting our country. What would Toni Smith do as other countries invade us? What would we *all* do as other militaries invade us, imprison us, rape women and abuse children.

It seems you can't turn on international news without hearing of a market square bomb explosion or innocent civilians being killed in a terrorist attack. How lucky we are that we can go to the grocery store or get on a bus without the fear that it will be blown to pieces.

Have you ever thought how incredibly blessed we are that we can live our life this way? No matter what you feel about the politics of our country, it is such a free and wonderful way of life that we do not have to live in the constant fear some other countries do.

> Our flag is a symbol of this.
> Our flag has been through a lot.
> Our flag should be respected.

"The strength of the United States is not the gold
at Fort Knox or the weapons of mass destruction
that we have, but the sum total of the education
and the character of our people"

—*Claiborne Pell (1918-)*[18]

*   *   *

The 21-Gun Salute witnessed at military funerals stands for the sum of the numbers in the year 1776. 1+7+7+6=21

FOLDING THE FLAG

The United States has many beautiful customs, the military in particular. While witnessing Ronald Reagan's funeral and the emotional flag folding ceremony, I watched tearfully, respecting that each fold has a meaning.

1st Fold—a symbol of life

2nd Fold—a symbol of our belief in eternal life

3rd Fold—in honor and remembrance of the veterans departing our ranks who gave a portion of their lives for the defense of our country to attain peace throughout the world

4th Fold—represents our weaker nature, for as American citizens trusting in God, it is to Him we turn in times of peace as well as in time of war for His divine guidance

5th Fold—a tribute to our country, for in the words of Stephen Decatur, "Our Country, in dealing with other countries, may she always be right; but it is still our country, right or wrong"

6th Fold—for where our hearts lie. It is with our heart that We pledge allegiance to the flag of the United States of America, and the Republic for which it stands, one Nation under God, Indivisible, with Liberty and Justice for all

7th Fold—a tribute to our Armed Forces, for it is through the Armed Forces that we protect our country and our flag against all her enemies, whether they be found within or without the boundaries of our Republic

8th Fold—a tribute to the one who entered into the valley of the shadow of death, that we might see the light of day.

9th Fold—a tribute to womanhood, and Mothers. For it has been through their faith, their love, loyalty and devotion that the character of the men and women who have made this country great has been molded

10th Fold—a tribute to the father, for he, too, has given his sons and daughters for the defense of our country since they were first born

11th Fold—represents the lower portion of the seal of King David and King Solomon and glorifies in the Hebrews eyes, the God of Abraham, Isaac and Jacob

12th Fold—represents an emblem of eternity and glorifies, in the Christians eyes, God the Father, the Son and Holy Spirit.

13th Fold—the flag is completely folded, the stars are uppermost reminding us of our nations motto, "In God We Trust"

The flag completely folded, takes on the appearance of a cocked hat. This is to remind us of the soldiers who served under General George Washington and the Sailors and Marines who served under Captain John Paul Jones, who were followed by their comrades and shipmates in the Armed Forces of the United States, preserving for us the rights, privileges and freedoms we enjoy today.

America has so many beautiful customs and traditions . . . let us preserve them.

* * *

"A love of tradition has never weakened a nation, indeed it has strengthened nations in their hour of peril;"

—*Sir Winston Churchill(1874-1965) on November 29, 1944 speech in the House of Commons*[19]

CHAPTER 3

OF THE UNITED STATES OF AMERICA

> "Sitting at the table doesn't make you a diner unless
> you eat some of what's on that plate. Being here in
> America doesn't make you an American. Being born
> here in America doesn't make you an American."

—*Malcolm X (1925-1965), Malcolm X Speaks, 1965*[1]

THE INGREDIENTS OF OUR "MELTING POT"

The United States enjoys the most diverse cultural society in the world, embracing descendants from every part of the globe. This unique cultural blend is arguably our most distinct characteristic, resulting in the catchphrase "Melting Pot". Even *The Statue Of Liberty* jumped on the Welcome Wagon Bandwagon. Given to us as a gift from France (thanks France, but next time could you please send Louis Vuitton purses?) she welcomes foreigners with her outstretched beacon of light.

Though Native American Indians hold bragging rights as the first-born Americans, only 92 percent of the total population was actually born in the United States. The largest foreign-born populations by country are Mexico, Cuba, Dominican Republic, El Salvador, Great Britain, China and Hong Kong, India, Korea, Philippines and Vietnam.[2] That is why Spanish is the most commonly spoken second-language in the United States. The U.S. Census also reports 10.7% of the U.S. population speaks Spanish at home and more than 30% of the population speaks a language other than English at home.

Out of the estimated 291,575,000 people in the United States, the **ancestry** breakdown goes something like this, according to the Bureau of the Census.[3]

ANCESTRY	PERSONS	% FOREIGN BORN
Albanian	38,361	32.8
American	13,039,560	0.1
Armenian	267,975	44.5
Assyrian	46,099	58.6
Australian	36,290	39.4
Austrian	545,856	11.2
Barbadian	33,178	74.6
Basque	37,842	14.2
Belgian	248,075	11.0
Belizean	21,205	75.3
Brazilian	57,108	72.5
British West Indian	35,822	79.5
Bulgarian	20,894	32.3
Cajun	597,729	0.1
Canadian	361,612	34.1
Cape Verdean	46,552	28.9
Croatian	409,458	7.5
Czech	772,087	3.7
Czechoslovakian	240,489	7.7
Danish	980,868	3.8
Dutch	3,475,410	3.6
Dutch West Indian	33,473	4.0
Egyptian	73,097	69.2
English	22,703,652	2.8
Estonian	20,996	47.5
Ethiopian	33,868	81.4
Finnish	465,070	4.8
French	6,204,184	2.7

French Canadian	1,698,394	6.7
German	45,583,932	1.8
Greek	921,782	21.0
Guyanese	75,765	85.3
Haitian	280,874	70.9
Hungarian	997,545	12.4
Icelander	27,171	20.2
Iranian	220,714	77.0
Iraqi	20,657	69.5
Irish	22,721,252	1.2
Israeli	69,018	56.6
Italian	11,286,815	5.7
Jamaican	410,933	72.8
Latvian	75,747	36.4
Lebanese	309,578	25.5
Lithuanian	526,089	6.6
Luxemburger	28,846	4.6
Maltese	30,292	30.4
Nigerian	86,875	55.5
Norwegian	2,517,760	1.9
Palestinian	44,65	1 56.9
Pennsylvania German	246461	0.2
Polish	6,542,844	6.2
Portuguese	900,060	25.8
Romanian	235,774	29.1
Russian	2,114,506	9.2
Scotch-Irish	4,334,197	0.7
Scottish	3,315,306	4.6
Serbian	89,583	21.5
Slavic	43,301	6.2
Slovak	1,210,652	3.3
Slovene	87,500	7.8
Swedish	2,881,950	2.0
Swiss	607,833	5.9
Syrian	95,155	23.4
Trinidadian/Tobagoni	71720	80.8
Turkish	66,492	53.5
Ukrainian	514,08	5 17.9
Welsh	1,038,603	1.7
Yugoslavian	184,952	25.3

Descent Vs. Nationality

Descent is the key word. It is important for Americans to appreciate their descent, but not confuse *descent* with *nationality*. Every American is unique in their descent, yet all share a common nationality. With the over 68 "ingredients" in our Melting Pot, nationalism is imperative if we are to cultivate as one nation.

ASIAN-AMERICAN/ IRISH-AMERICAN/ MEXICAN—AMERICAN/CAN'T WE JUST SAY "AMERICAN"?

I am an "Ellis Island Grandchild". My grandfather came to this country over one century ago. He passed Lady Liberty, like so many of our ancestors, with nothing but hope and a dream for prosperity. Although he raised his family with a sense of ancestral culture, my grandfather was clearly an 'American'. With his newfound citizenship came a newfound loyalty. He did not run up to Washington to lobby on behalf of his birth country or make his money here, only to send it to relatives back in the "old country". He was an American and very proud of his new homeland.

LAND OF OPPORTUNITY OR LAND OF OPPORTUNISTS?

I am sad how few immigrants there are today like my grandfather. I have met too many foreigners who work here in the United States and enjoy milking our system. Take what they can get from Uncle Sam, all the while their loyalty is with their homeland. It is essential to be part of a global economy on an economic standpoint. But, our lawmakers need to look into why other countries are prospering while our economy is weakening in this wonderful "global economy" of ours.

An alarming statistic by the *Bureau of the Census* and *Bureau of Economic Analysis* reports imports increased more than exports with the nation's international deficit in goods and services increasing from $42.1 billion in February to $46 billion in March of 2004.[4] An increase of $4 billion in only two months? No wonder we don't see much of those labels *Made In U.S.A* anymore. The labels now silently read *Used To Be Made In U.S.A. But Man It's Cheaper To Make It In China!* Has Congress bothered to pass effective tax incentive laws to keep factories here at home? Nope. Nada. Nothing. The sad part is, in the end, countries like China will be the big winner and we will be the big loser.

I was also saddened when a friend of mine, who is a cotton farmer, was having financial problems. When I asked him what was wrong, he said, "Our country subsidizes Egypt's cotton. I can't compete."

What is wrong with this picture? We are economically helping a country who, as history tells me, hates our guts, while our own go broke? The answer to that is at the end of this chapter.

HEY LAWMAKERS! CHARITY STARTS AT HOME!

The legislators who represent these farm states should be ashamed of themselves. How do they sleep at night knowing they pass laws giving international aid that inevitably hurt our own fellow Americans? Stop depending on Willie Nelson and all the wonderful entertainers who perform at *Farm-Aid* helping the farmers the best they can.

Willie Nelson for Congress!

It is comforting, though, that the frustration with Congress has lasted well over two-hundred years. Maybe future legislators can change this image?

COMMENTS ON CONGRESS[5]

"Oh, I don't blame Congress. If I had $600 million at my disposal, I'd be irresponsible, too."

—Lichty and Wagner

"It could probably be shown by facts and figures that there is no distinctly American criminal class except Congress."

—Mark Twain (1835-1910)

"Congress consists of one third, more or less, scoundrels; two thirds, more or less idiots; and three thirds, more or less, poltroons.

—H.L.Mencken (1880-1956)

"Suppose you were an idiot and suppose you were a member of Congress. But I repeat myself."

—Mark Twain (1835-1910)

"I don't mind what Congress does, as long as they don't do it in the streets and frighten the horses."

—Victor Hugo (1802-1885)

"This country has come to feel the same when Congress is in session as when the baby gets hold of a hammer."

—Will Rogers (1879-1935)

"After two years in Washington, I often long for the realism and sincerity of Hollywood."

—Fred Thompson, in a speech before the
Commonwealth Club of California

MONROE DOCTRINE, MONROE DOCTRINE-WHERE FOR ART THOU?

Remember the Monroe Doctrine? President James (yep, you got it) Monroe introduced it to Congress on December 2, 1823. It maintained the nations of the Western Hemisphere against European interference "for the purpose of oppressing them or controlling in any other manner their destiny." Also, that American contents were "henceforth not to be considered as subjects for future colonization by any European powers".[6] The underlying theme being—no new colonies to be created in America and no existing colonies were allowed to extend their boundaries.

Well, living on a Texas border town where Cinco de Mayo gets as much attention as the Fourth of July, I can't help but wonder if the Monroe Doctrine needs to be enforced again.

The Monroe Doctrine has rarely flexed its muscle, and has hardly been imposed. When England was in a dispute over Oregon, President James Polk exercised it in 1845 and President Grover Cleveland used it later to threaten England over a challenge with Venezuela in 1895. It surfaced once more in the 1860's during the French intervention in Mexico.[7]

And as for my cotton farmer friends, the Monroe Doctrine prohibits other countries "controlling in any other manner their destiny" and since another country *is* controlling their livelihood, it appears the Monroe Doctrine has been violated. Although this example is a bit extreme, it is not extremism in wondering, "Where will America finally draw the line?" Is it time to get the Monroe Doctrine back into America's Gym and reflex its' muscle?

FOREIGN-AID
MORAL OBLIGATION OR FOREIGN POLICY?

Quiz—What percentage of the United States' annual budget is spent on foreign aid?

   A. 1%
   B. 5%
   C. 10%
   D. 24%

A poll in 2001 sponsored by the University of Maryland showed that most Americans think the United States spends about 24 % of its annual budget on foreign aid.[8]

Answer to quiz:
A. Less than 1%.

Did you pick A? Or did you pick D for Dummies . . . because that's what we are unless we track exactly where our money is going.

Many Americans feel "How can we give money to other countries when we have our own people starving and homeless?" To that I say AMEN! That's why I was so surprised to learn such a small portion of the U.S. budget goes to foreign aid. Kind of reminds you of that rich uncle that no one knew was rich until after he died and left millions of dollars in his will, huh? Well, fellow Americans, we all have that rich uncle and his name is Uncle Sam.

UNCLE SAM'S KIDS-The Rich Cousins

Just like foreign aid, the *real motive* behind charitable contributions is also questionable.Are private donations subject to special interest? Is it sincere charity or 'cheers to me'? Let's take a look.

In November of 2004, Bill Gates announced a donation to India for $100 million over ten years to help in the fight of AIDS. During that time, he made another contribution, this time for a three year span of over $400 million, to increase support for Microsoft's development of applications and its platforms.[9] Keep in mind, Linux and other computer industry competition was spreading across that part of the world. So, what was Bill Gates' motive . . . AIDS or Microsoft-AID? Whether the motive was greedy or not, I sincerely hope the AIDS money finds more purpose.

These days, I suppose no one gives without getting something in return.

PEEKING INTO THE WORLD'S CHECKBOOKS

Back to foreign aid. In raw dollars, the United States is the top donor, but the foreign-aid budget as a percentage of the gross national product ranks last among the world's wealthiest countries. For more than a decade Japan was up on us in this department. Even the Netherlands gave $3.2 billion in 2001 . . . that is almost a third of what the big bad U.S. donated.

FOREIGN AID-2001[10]
$10.9 billion—United States
$9.7 billion—Japan
$4.9 billion—Germany
$4.7 billion—England
$4.3 billion—France

But, in terms of GNP, the top countries were Denmark, Norway, Netherlands, Luxembourg and Sweden.

p.s. During the Reagan administration, foreign aid was

a critical tool in containing communism during the Cold War. Aid reached $27 billion per year. (almost three times the current level)[11]

HEADS—Israel Gets It
TAILS—Egypt Gets It

The U.S. Agency of International Development maintains that "U.S. foreign assistance has always had the twofold purpose of furthering America's foreign policy interests in expanding democracy and free markets while improving the lives of the citizens of the developing world."[12]

Yet, the biggest argument of critics is that the U.S. gives aid to reward political partners more than it does to advance humanitarian causes abroad. What do you think? Are we giving because we are charitable Americans or are we giving because that country has a military base with beachfront property baby! You know, it's your tax dollars being taken overseas . . . Aren't you curious as to who gets it?

How in the world do we decide which countries get it and how much?

I was picturing a check that looks like this—

Pay To The Order   **Date:** For Frickin' Ever
Country Who Supports Democracy

Amount A couple of billion dollars

Memo: have a nice day_____*The President of the U.S._*

But, in reality, the money goes indirectly through funding international organizations such as the United Nations, the World Bank, and the International Monetary

Fund.[13] Wow! I'd like to see the financial statements of those institutions!

PEEKING INTO THE U.S. CHECKBOOK

Let's see the countries that are benefiting from our April 15th tax returns

#1 ISRAEL
$2.1 billion in military aid
$600 million in economic support—

#2 EGYPT
$1.3 billion in military aid
$615 million in social programs—

#3 COLOMBIA
$540 million to battle drug trade and crack down on local terrorist groups—

#4 JORDAN
$250 million economic support
$198 million in military financing

#5 PERU/ UKRAINE/ RUSSIA
$200 million a piece in economic and military aid[14]

Since September 11th, the United States has increased funding to several pivotal countries strategically stemming from the War on Terror. Pakistan, Afghanistan, Turkey, Uzbekistan and Kyrgyzstan are such countries.[15]

I wonder how Israel and Egypt shot to the top of the list and I'm sure Australia is wondering the same thing! My guess is it has something to do with turning on the TV in 1979 and watching Jimmy Carter, Muhammed Anwar al-Sadat and Menahem Begin shaking hands and smiling over something. Remember that? It was the Camp David Accords, the Peace Treaty between Egypt and Israel which called for Israel's withdrawal from Sinai and the establishment of Palestinian autonomy in exchange for peace and normal relations with Egypt.[16]

* * *

The Shangri-La Accords?

If you get in good with the Prez, go to Camp David!

Camp David is the official retreat of the president of the United States. It is about 70 miles from Washington, D.C. nestled high in the Catoctin Mountains of Maryland. President Roosevelt established it as a presidential getaway in 1942. He named it 'Shangri-La', after the ideal mountain kingdom in James Hilton's book, *The Lost Horizon*. It was President Dwight D. Eisenhower who later renamed it Camp David in 1953, after his grandson David.[17]

* * *

So what's the answer . . . is it foreign policy or moral obligation? Probably a little of both.

Most wealthy nations give . . . whatever the underlying purpose may be.

* * *

"America is a large friendly dog in a very small room.
Every time it wags its tail, it knocks over a chair."

Arnold Toynbee (1889-1975)[18]

CHAPTER 4

AND TO THE REPUBLIC

"Television has proved that people will look at anything rather than each other."

—*Ann Landers (1918-2002)*[1]

THE MEDIA

Art imitates life. It is that simple. If you think back on the popularity of various shows, it is a clear reflection of the times. I grew up with *The Cosby Show*. No I didn't. I'm lying about my age again. I actually grew up, come on fingers, you can type it . . . with . . . . (age alert) *The Brady Bunch*. The worst thing I experienced as a child was when Marsha Brady broke her nose. I loved *The Partridge Family* and learned from that one episode that tomato juice gets rid of a skunk smell. My neighbors and I would play *Charlie's Angels*. They were suspenseful episodes with no blood and guts and the bad guy always lost.

Then there were the 80's, a time in history when shoulder pads were as big as egos. That saying "He Who Dies With The Most Toys Wins" seemed to be the silent national anthem. With shows like *Dynasty* and *Dallas*, our country was mesmerized with wealth and power. Ronald Reagan's "Reaganomics" Policy put more money in the hands of taxpayers and we loved it. Truly, the birth of the "30,000 A Year Millionaire". I was right in front of the television when MTV previewed for the first time in August of 1981. Doug Ferrari stated that "MTV is the lava lamp of the 1980's[1]" and video jockeys (VJ's) were far more interesting to watch than listening to disc jockeys (DJ's). Poor old DJ's were placed right up there with our eight-track tapes. We were such a self-centered society and the world was hating us for it. Even the "Love Everyone" era from the 60's Hippie and 70's Disco Era was being replaced by the angry Punk Rockers of the 80's.

Art was imitating life and we weren't tuning in.

> "We must never forget that art is not a form of propaganda; it is a form of truth."
>
> —*John F. Kennedy, October 26, 1963*[3]

Is anyone ashamed of the entertainment "glamorous Hollywood" provides? I am dreading the day when I am in the park with my child and other children "vote him off the playground" like we adults "vote each other off an island" like the television show *Survivor*. Columbine horrified us. We cannot understand when there are students killing in our schools yet, with movies like *Natural Born Killers* and *The Matrix*, we are the adults who provide similar actions in film and television productions. We accept it when the almighty dollar is involved, but reject it when society imitates it.

Adults need to put kids, not wallets, as a first priority. I wonder how the executives who approve making horrible, bloody, and terrorist-themed movies sleep at night. If you think there is nothing wrong with it then I pose this question to you. Why did the Arnold Schwarzenegger movie *Collateral Damage* put off its release because "they" felt it was too similar to September 11th and would be *"disturbing"*. Hello? Anybody out there?

This movie should be *"disturbing"* anyway!

p.s. I am curious to know who "they" is. You know, the "they" who felt it would be disturbing. I wonder if it's the same "they" my mother always referred to when she said things like, "They say eating broccoli is good for you".

"They" drives me nuts.

MEDIA ALERT MEDIA ALERT

This is my problem with the media. Everyone knows where O.J. Simpson's black glove was found on the Brentwood property, but not many know the last five laws passed by Congress. Media has a responsibility to inform me, the viewer, and this is the best they can come up with? Tabloid television has opened the window of our country looking like idiots, and everyone around the world is peeking in that window and laughing at us, not with us.

I hope *The Jerry Springer Show* one day regrets how ridiculous it made our society look. People on that show looked like fools with no self respect. Their "five minutes of fame" is the only reason I can guess why people would publicly humiliate themselves. Hey you! Yeah, you four-hundred pound tattoo lady that mothered a child by her husbands' brothers boss' secretary's neighbor, did you *really* need to come on national television? Ok, the episodes weren't that bad, but, it is suffice to say my fellow Americans were stripped of their dignity and I am sad for them. I am sure Jerry Springer was only doing his job as a host, but wait! Why did he put his name on the title of the show? Oops, sorry Jerry. I cannot excuse you either. By the way: Have you noticed that the camera always seems to mysteriously get "knocked down" during the fights on the *Jerry Springer Show* so you don't actually see the fight in its entirety?

*   *   *

"Television enables you to be entertained in your home
by people you wouldn't have in your home."

—*David Frost*[4]

Let's face it. We adults are selfish. Here is an example.
When *Barney the Dinosaur* shot to fame, every young child
was mesmerized. I could not help but notice how this
show seemed to contribute in making children more kind,
cooperative, sensitive; all characteristics we wish for in
our children. I was around a group of adults who were
talking about how Barney was the household favorite
with their small children when one father said, "Barney,
oh that show is so stupid!" I told him, "Well, I sure hope
you think Barney is stupid at your age. I would really be
worried if you enjoyed it as a grown man!" Do you see?
There we go again.

The "It's All About Me" mentality.

If you disagree then why don't we do this . . . why don't
we make a law for divorced couples that *they* have to go
back and forth every other weekend and change houses
instead of dragging their kids back and forth?

Oh, because it's too inconvenient right?

I rest my case.

*   *   *

"The thing that impresses me most about
America is the way parents obey their children."

—*King Edward VIII (1894-1972)*[5]

ON THE FLIP SIDE

Just as we should demand more from the media, the
media should demand more from us.

If Tom Brokaw shows me the picture above and tells me it is a picture of a man sitting beside a tree, should I believe him? No, I should not. I should take the picture presented to me and study the facts. From those facts I may draw my *own* conclusion that "No Tom. That picture is not of a man beside a tree, but of a boy beside a bush."

So, what is it? a man or a boy? A tree or a bush? Let's get even more complicated and say it is a democratic tree or a republican bush (no pun intended). When Tom Brokaw reports a man, bush, boy, tree . . . who is right? I get a kick out of people who say "The Liberal Press" or "Conservative Journalism". If I were a Libertarian, you would have said, "Ugh! Those Libertarians think that is a tree"!

So, how can we achieve the impossible feat of being objective? That is where we, as viewers, need to take all information presented to us and further our knowledge through research and come up with the facts ourselves. Remember, most documented history about Katherine the

Great of Russia was written by her enemies. Objective? I don't think so. So the main point? The point is there is no such thing as "objective journalism" so get over it.

We must look at all angles and draw our own intelligent conclusions. We are humans with a brain, not robots that need to be programmed. Wait! Do you think that is why they're called television "programs"?

We are living creatures with the innate ability to reason. So, let's use it!

Look at both sides of the coin
You will be richer for it

"Television is a new medium. It's called a medium because nothing is well-done."

—*Fred Allen (1894-1956)* [6]

CAPITALISM GONE WILD

Joe Francis. Does that name ring a bell? No? Let me try again. Ever heard of *Girls Gone Wild* videos? Well, Joe Francis is every parent who has a daughter's worst nightmare. Joe Francis is the brainchild behind *Girls Gone Wild*.

If I were a girl in one of the videos, I'd be furious that my body bought the private jet and multi-million dollar lifestyle he so arrogantly enjoys. If the girls are doing this on their own free-will, I ask Joe Francis this: If this is the case, why is it being done in such a heavy alcohol-atmosphere? I would believe him more if the girls flashed, say, coming out of the supermarket, or walking in the park with their dog, but, not partying hard. . . . sorry Joe, it just doesn't fly.

Maybe I'm just picking on Joe because women, like me, were stripped (literally and figuratively) of their dignity. Maybe I'm bitter because there is not a video series of men for ME to enjoy. Regardless, I wonder why he didn't have *his* female relatives in the videos . . .

hmmm . . . I smell double-standard. Many American women are sad for Arab women who, as tradition has it, must wear burkas. Well, as oppressive as it seems, at least there is not a cocky Mohammad-Joe Al-Francis living it up and making millions on other women's embarrassment. However, on an economic standpoint and out of respect for entrepreneurship in this country, that creep Joe Francis found a niche in society and capitalized on it . . . God Bless America.

> "Nobody ever went broke underestimating the taste of the American public."

> —H.L. Menchen (1880-1956)[7]

Move over Joe Francis. It's time for . . .

"SALARIES GONE WILD"

The American dollar just doesn't seem to mean much anymore. Millionaires are poverty-level next to billionaires. Even the game show *Who Wants To Be A Millionaire* got shunned for *Super Millionaire* because winning a million bucks just didn't cut it. I miss the old days when *Match Game '77* host Gene Rayburn would hold his long skinny microphone and engage in friendly banter with the cast. Everyone was genuinely happy for the person that won $1,500! Remember the *Newlywed Game*? The couple would be so excited to win, "your very own, brand new, stereo!"

Fasten Your Seat Belt—

We are about to drive through the ridiculous of professional sports.

Forbes Magazine had a fascinating article *World's 50*

Highest Paid Athletes in their July 5, 2004 issue and listed the best-paid athletes of 2004. The extensive list is a combination of salaries, winnings, endorsements, appearance fees and other revenue. [8]

Here are the Top Five:

1: Tiger Woods, Golfer
   - Total Earnings: $80.3 million
   Almost 70 million stems from endorsements.
2: Michael Schumacher, Race Car Driver
   - Total Earnings: $80 million
   Ferrari provides him an annual salary of 40 million.
3: Peyton Manning, Football—Indianapolis Colts
   - Total Earnings: $42 million
   Only 4 NFL players made the top 50, but Manning's was the largest signing bonus in the history of team sports at $34.5 million.
4: Michael Jordan, Basketball-retired
   - Total Earnings: $35 million
   Nike alone provides him with 25 million a year.
5: Shaquille O'Neal, L.A. Lakers
   - Total Earnings: $31.9 million
   He is the highest paid pro basketball player.

According to Forbes Magazine, basketball had fourteen players on the list, more than any other team sport. Baseball came in second with thirteen players.[9]

TIME-OUT

Do you think NFL really stands for **No Financial Leverage?** *Tall kids need apply. Forget football, the money is in the NBA.*

And kudos to Tiger Woods. Let me pull out my calculator . . . 3 . . . plus . . . 8 . . . carry the 1 . . . divide by 6 . . . wow! It's worth about 10 million to play good golf and about 70 million to have a good personality!

GO GOLF!

You have to admire individual sports like golf and tennis, because unlike team sports, players are paid in direct proportion with how well they play.

But, is it true that Golf really stands for GENTLEMAN ONLY LADIES FORBIDDEN? Nah! The word 'golf' actually comes from the Dutch word 'colf', which means 'club'.

*   *   *

"Although golf was originally restricted to
wealthy, overweight Protestants, today it's open
to anybody who owns hideous clothing."

—*Dave Barry*[10]

GOLF AND THE MEDIA

You have to crack up how the media overexposes certain athletes. One of the most overexposed coverage in all of sports has to be the way the media covers the PGA and Tiger Woods. This guy could be last and the media can't get enough of him!

"And we have Fred Couples in the lead with -8. But, let's go over to Tiger Woods whose at +11. And Tiger Woods is on the green in 3 and it's a par 3! What a shot! Back over to Ernie Els who is also tied for the lead with Couples at -8 who just chipped in for an eagle. But back to Tiger Woods! Even though he's in 17th place at the moment, look at that amazing shot out of the sand! Els is tied for the lead but back now to another South African, Tim Clark whose tied for second at the moment with fellow countryman Rotief Goosen, but wait! Let's go back to Tiger Woods! He's now in 16th place! Tiger is amazing! Goosen just had a 'hole-in-one' but who cares because Tiger is now in 15th place!"

The best players should have the media spotlight . . . period.

USE YOUR HEAD WHEN YOU USE YOUR WALLET

Prices in professional sports have turned into one big joke. Every time we pay for that emblem on a baseball cap, or outrageous prices for NBA tickets, it's really we the consumer, not the professional sports organizations, that are getting the short end of the stick. And who is really, really getting the short end of the stick? It's Average Joe. Average Joe who is shelling out his hard-earned cash. A big contrast from Big Corporate Joe, who can afford those outrageous prices and probably writes them off as a company expense anyway.

BASEBALL, HOTDOGS, APPLE PIE AND MONEY

> "If it weren't for baseball, many kids wouldn't
> know what a millionaire looked like."
>
> —*Phyllis Diller*[11]

The deal between the Texas Rangers and the New York Yankees is probably the craziest of all. Alex Rodriguez was traded to the Yankee's, right? The Rangers had to pay $67 million of the $179 million left on Rodriguez's $252 million 10-year contract.

True, the Rangers got two players in return (one is an All-Star), but they also will pay Rodriguez through 2025.[12]

It was the most cash included in a trade in major league history. Commissioner Bud Selig approved the record-setting deal stating, "I am very concerned about the large amount of cash consideration involved in the transaction, and the length of time over which the cash is being paid,". He continued, "I want to make it abundantly clear to all clubs that I will not allow cash transfers of this magnitude to become the norm. However, given the unique circumstances, including the size, length and complexity of Mr. Rodriguez's contract and the quality of the talent moving in both directions, I have decided to approve the transaction."[13]

Unique circumstances, Bud? I don't buy it. I was so upset when a Japanese corporation bought Rockefeller Center. It was an American symbol and we somehow got 'sold out'. Well, here it goes again. Baseball is the *one* American symbol that the Japanese didn't buy out, but why should they?

Bud Selig did it for them.

*   *   *

"You can tell the ideals of a nation by its advertisements."

—*Norman Douglas*[14]

PLEASE PAUSE FOR THIS COMMERCIAL BREAK

Product: LaFresh Soap

1970's Commercial For Lafresh Soap—

"New! LaFresh Soap.

The fresh scent will leave you ready for peace-activist protests by day and a groovy evening of disco dancing by night! LaFresh Soap is available in 3 scents:

1. Wanna-Be-David-Cassidy-Watermelon
2. Crosby, Stills and Nutmeg Spice
3. Fresh Fonzie from Happy Days.

Far-out! Let's make peace-not war and buy a bar of LaFresh Soap today! Official soap of the Bionic Woman.

1980's Commercial For LaFresh Soap—

"New and Improved LaFresh Soap and Diet-LaFresh Soap

'Millionaires' who make $30,000 a year can't resist the fresh scent. You can even use it on the leather of your brand-new BMW convertible! This company has great stock options and is listed on the Forbes Best 100 Soap List.

LaFresh Soap is available in 3 expensive scents:

1. Pine Scent Like My Second Home in Aspen
2. Lamborghini Lemon
3. Yuppies and Cream

Even punk rock bands use LaFresh to spike their mohawk hair styles. Great for mullets too! Awesome! If you look inside the wrapper, there's a tax-incentive program if you make over $100,000 a year. Official soap of J.R. Ewing.

1990's Commercial For LaFresh Soap

"Recyclable, Ecological, Non-Animal Tested LaFresh Soap.

Lathers well with bottled water. Make grunge smell good after a hard day of rollerblading with 3 new fresh scents:

1. Musty-Millionaires Be Gone
2. Hillary Thinks She's President Honeydew
   Also available: Honeydew This and Honey Pass—My—Healthcare—Plan—That Coconut
3. Impeach Clinton Peach.

After you build up a sweat fighting road rage, LaFresh will ease your tension so you can continue to email, page, text message, instant message, fax, or call-wait/forward/ or three-way call your stress away!

LaFresh Soap is especially safe for colored-contact lenses, soft disposable contacts, liposuction, collagen lip injections, breast implants, chemical peels, skin laser resurfacing and laser hair removal. No check or cash payment is accepted, but you may use your credit or debit card to purchase LaFresh Soap. Official soap of the *Saved By The Bell* kids before the college years.

2000's Commercial For LaFresh Soap

"Adkin's—Friendly LaFresh Soap.

Effectively washes away the Y2K Millenium Bug. Microsoft has just come out with Scents 2000, but you must buy their PC in order to activate the program.

1. "Rose-Ceremony" Rose
2. Wazzup-Peace-Out-Fools-Strawberry
3. Ricky Martin Rasberry.

Unfortunately, there are no more choices where you buy LaFresh because Wal-Mart has put every store out of business. You can now only shop at Wal-Mart and Sam's Club. Sam's Club offers LaFresh in 32, 64 or 96 count-sets. If you have a problem with that, please contact the ACLU. The ACLU is currently suing LaFresh for religious connotations when a man shouted, "God I feel clean" after using the soap. The case is under appeal.

LaFresh Soap has no official sponsor and does not discriminate on the basis of color, sex, race or religion.

*   *   *

This is the end of chapter four . . . would you like fries with that?

*   *   *

CHAPTER 5

FOR WHICH IT STANDS

"I'm not sure I want popular opinion on my side-I've noticed those with the most opinions often have the fewest facts."

—Bethania McKenstry[1]

CeleBRATies

It should be spelled "celebraty" instead of "celebrity", because many of them are just that. Brats! . . . Jessica Lange, George Clooney, Susan Sarandon, Michael Moore, Janeane Garofalo, Martin Sheen and many others.

How many of them actually wrote their Congressman or even educated themselves on a political issue before they rushed to the camera spotlight?

In fairness, many stars *do* realize that a celebrity spokesman is not ideal. Actor Jason Priestly said, "I think more people should keep their opinions to themselves" and Ron Silver pointed out many of his fellow celebrities cannot control the media publicizing their political views, " . . . because at the end of the day, who cares? There are more important things on the table. But, if they wanted to use Natialie Maines or Tim Robbins or me, or whomever, that's their business." [2]

But, perhaps Robert Duvall said it best of all. "They should keep their mouths shut." [3]

*   *   *

"The media just loves to pay attention to whatever is happening that makes the most noise."

Kelsey Grammer [4]

Okay Media criticized in chapter 4, gotta point the
finger on you! After all, you're the ones who provide that
camera spotlight. It's not just television media either, it's
the movie and print industry as well.

Liberals always seem to get the blame for driving a
wedge that divides this country further and further apart.
I always thought that was unfair until . . . enter Michael
Moore. An egocentric who apparently has no respect for
the fact that our country is at war. War means that as a
country, we stand behind our Commander-In-Chief. War
means we honor our Army, Navy, Air Force, Marines, and
National Guard. War means we come together with
patriotic solidarity as a nation. In fairness, maybe no one
told Michael Moore we are in war. What's worse . . . maybe
someone did and he ate them.

As a "once-a-fat-kid-always-a-fat-kid" adult, that was
mean, I'll admit. But now, at least Michael Moore will know
what it feels like to be attacked unfairly. Hezbollah and
other groups who hate America praised his film, and that
was enough for me. Back in the pioneer days, people like
Moore were tried for treason and shot at sunrise. Today,
people like Moore make millions and millions of dollars
doing a smear campaign on our country and are praised
by Liberals for doing so. The next time you think about the
money you spent to see that propaganda disguised as a
movie, remember the damage it has done to our country is
irreparable. And the image he gave our soldiers is unfair.

If Moore were such a great American, he would have
joined the CIA or FBI and investigated President Bush and
conducted a formal investigation. Or he would have

donated the hundreds of millions of dollars the movie grossed to a worthwhile, non-partisan charity. Instead, he got rich off of you and me and we are stuck with the bad impression he portrayed all around the world, as he is laughing all the way to the bank.

We need to get pride back in our country. It is fine to challenge the status quo, but we seem to point the finger at everyone but ourselves. What's worse, people like Moore use their celebrity to point the finger at any political party that is not their own.

Michael Moore needs to have a second look at our nation's creed. Do you think he even knows we have a creed?

THE AMERICAN'S CREED
by William Tyler Page

"I believe in the United States of America as a government of the people, by the people, for the people; whose just powers are derived from the consent of the governed, a democracy in a republic, a sovereign Nation of many sovereign States; a perfect union, one and inseparable; established upon those principles of freedom, equality, justice, and humanity for which American patriots sacrificed their lives and fortunes. "I therefore believe it is my duty to my country to love it, to support its Constitution, to obey its laws to respect its flag, and to defend it against all enemies."

—*Written 1917, accepted by the United States House of Representatives on April 3, 1918*

The American's Creed states, *I therefore believe it is my duty to my country to love it*. Michael Moore clearly proved he does not love my country. *And to defend it against all enemies.* Instead of against all enemies, he chose to defend the enemy. Game's over Michael. You trashed the home team. Disqualified.

PAY ATTENTION HOLLYWOOD BECAUSE YOU MISSED THE POINT

> "People often demand freedom of speech as a
> compensation for the freedom of thought which
> they seldom use."
>
> —Soren Kierkegaard (1813-1855)[5]

Do you remember when Tim Robbins spoke of a 'McCarthyism" feel in speaking out against the War in Iraq? Americans do not want to deny anyone the right to free speech. What's upsetting is when our television time is wasted on a celebrity speaking out against something that is not their expertise. You can turn on any cable news network and find opposition to the War in Iraq all day long, but under their name is usually a respected title such *as PH.D, New York University,* or *Professor International Studies.* Of course everyone is allowed the right to speak their mind, but why don't they do it at a neighborhood meeting, grocery store or even in the office of their local elected officials? Just don't do it on my sixty-dollar-a-month cable bill time!

There is so much going on that we, civilians, do not know. I doubt that Martin Sheen ever sat in on Defense Department or CIA meetings. The guy plays a president on television and suddenly thinks he's an expert! To speak out against something you have little or no knowledge about is ludicrous. That gripe from Hollywood that there was a sense of "McCarthyism" for their speaking out against the war really wasn't the main issue. The public was not shunning you out of a "McCarthyism" spirit, but because you somehow felt your opinion should be voiced louder than the Average Joe.

Many were irritated that certain celebrities aired their dirty political laundry on foreign soil. Not what they said, it was just plain common sense that it was an inappropriate venue. The Dixie Chicks plucked around in England, Michael Moore chose France, while Jessica Lange chose Spain as her "Bash—My-Country—Getaway". Cowardly, cowardly, cowardly.

> "When I am abroad, I always make it a rule never to criticize or attack the government of my own country. I make up for lost time when I come home."
>
> —*Sir Winston Churchill (1874-1965)*[6]

Closing message, it's not about denying the right to free speech. It is about showing class, dignity and a little respect for a country that has given you one heck of a life!

Get to the head of the class by showing class

WHAT IS THE LOUDEST, MOST EFFECTIVE WAY TO PROTEST?

VOTE!

Protestors: No one is bothered *that* you protest, it's *how* you protest. Protest to your civic leaders and you will earn more respect. Speaking of respect, when you protest, think about the men and women in uniform who are defending your life, a total stranger. Holding up anti-war signs doesn't make their job any easier. Because of our military we are safe nation.

No Draft . . . Brave Soldiers By Choice

It is truly amazing to have a country that no longer institutes the draft, because there are enough brave men and women who are willing to put their life on the line and courageously defend our country.

During the election year, The War On Terror was a hot political issue. What an insult when some politicians were using it as a political weapon saying, "We're sending your children off to war". We're sending your children off to war? It sounds like we kidnap sixth-graders, dress them up like soldiers and hand them an AK47 and ship them off to the Middle East! Of course, our military is composed of someone's 'children' . . . as well as someone's brother, sister, mother, father, uncle, aunt, grandfather or friend. But, the United States forces are not 'children.' They are highly equipped, highly trained professionals who deserve more respect than to be called 'children'.

Respect those who protect you or you really don't deserve to be protected.

That is how we have become a free nation, through war.

"We make war that we may live in peace."

—*Aristotle (384 BC-322 BC) Nichomachean Ethics* [7]

One thing that makes us a unique and wonderful country is our peaceful transfer of power. Have you ever marveled how amazing Inauguration Day is in that it does not bring about fighting and violence? Even if we did not vote for the president that will be sworn into office, it is a beautiful ceremony to witness every four years. This miraculous diplomatic transfer of leadership and support of whoever is in the Oval Office is essential in maintaining democracy. Maybe you cringed for Clinton's eight years in office or critical of Bush's term, but, in a democracy we respect them nonetheless because they are the leader of the Executive Branch and The Commander-in-Chief of the Armed Forces of the United States of America. After witnessing our country on September 11th, we have shown the ability to be more united than ever.

FYI . . .

The Great Seal (you see it on the podium when the President speaks) shows a bald eagle holding an olive branch and arrows. Do you know what the olive branch and arrows stand for? The olive branch symbolizes a desire for peace. The arrows symbolize the ability to wage war.

Meaning, the United States has a desire for peace, yet the ability to wage war. [8]

EMPLOYMENT OPPORTUNITY- EDUCATION AND EXPERIENCE NECESSARY

"I not only use all the brains that I have, but all that I can borrow"

—President Woodrow Wilson (1856-1924)[9]

Here is a brief synopsis of the Resumes of Political Leaders: [10]

William J. Clinton, Former President of the United States:
Degree from Georgetown University
Rhodes Scholarship to Oxford University
Law Degree from Yale University
Attorney General of Arkansas
Governor of Arkansas

George W. Bush, President of the United States:

Bachelors Degree from Yale University
MBA from Harvard Business School.
Governor of Texas

Dick Cheney, Vice President of the United States:
B.A. in political science
M.A. in political science
A staff member during the presidency of Richard Nixon
White House chief of staff under Gerald Ford
Elected to the House of Representatives from Wyoming in
    1978
Served as vice chairman of the committee investigating the
    Iran-Contra scandal under Ronald Reagan
Secretary of Defense under George Bush, a major role
    during the Gulf War

Secretary of State Colin Powell:
B.S. Geology CCNY
M.B.A. George Washington University
Recipient of two Presidential Medals of Freedom, the
    President's Citizens Medal, the Congressional Gold
    Medal, the Secretary of State Distinguished Service
    Medal, and the Secretary of Energy Distinguished
    Service Medal.

Donald Rumsfeld, Secretary of Defense :
Attended Princeton University on Scholarship A.B.
Served in the U.S. Navy (1954-57) as a Naval aviator
Congressional Assistant to Rep. Robert Griffin (R-MI), 1957-59
U.S. Representative, Illinois, 1962-69
Assistant to the President, Director of the Office of Economic
    Opportunity, Director of the Cost of Living
Council, 1969-74
U.S. Ambassador to NATO, 1973-74
Head of Presidential Transition Team, 1974

Assistant to the President, Director of White House Office
    of Operations
White House Chief of Staff, 1974-77
Secretary of Defense, 1975-77

Tom Ridge, Secretary of Homeland Security:
Scholarship to Harvard, graduating with honors in 1967
After his first year at The Dickinson School of Law, drafted
    into the U.S. Army, infantry staff sergeant in Vietnam,
    earning the Bronze Star for Valor.
Finished Law Degree and was in private practice before
    becoming Assistant District Attorney in Erie County.
Elected to Congress in 1982
First enlisted Vietnam combat veteran elected to the U.S.
    House, and was re-elected six times

Condoleezza Rice, National Security Advisor:
Bachelor's Degree in Political Science, Cum Laude and Phi
    Beta Kappa, the University of Master's from the
    University of Notre Dame
Ph.D. from the Graduate School of International Studies at
    the University of Denver
A Fellow of the American Academy of Arts and Sciences
Honorary Doctorates from Morehouse College in 1991, the
    University of Alabama in 1994, and the University of
    Notre Dame
At Stanford, a member of the Center for International
    Security and Arms Control
Senior Fellow of the Institute for International Studies
Fellow (by courtesy) of the Hoover Institution
From 1989 through March 1991, the period of German
    reunification and the final days of the Soviet Union,
    she served in the Bush Administration as Director, and
    then Senior Director, of Soviet and East

European Affairs in the National Security Council, and a
 Special Assistant to the President for National
Security Affairs
In 1986, while an international affairs fellow of the Council
 on Foreign Relations, she served as Special
Assistant to the Director of the Joint Chiefs of Staff.
In 1997, served on the Federal Advisory Committee on
 Gender—Integrated Training in the Military
A member of the boards of directors for the Chevron
 Corporation, the Charles Schwab Corporation, the
William and Flora Hewlett Foundation, the University of
 Notre Dame, the International Advisory
Council of J.P. Morgan
Vice President of the Boys and Girls Club of the Peninsula
Past board service with organizations such as: Transamerica
 Corporation, Hewlett Packard, the Carnegie
Corporation, Carnegie Endowment for International Peace,
 The Rand Corporation, the
National Council for Soviet and East European Studies, the
 Mid-Peninsula Urban Coalition and KQED, public
 broadcasting for San Francisco
Fellow of the American Academy of Arts and Sciences

Brief Synopsis: Education of Outspoken Celebrities:[11]

Alec Baldwin: Attended George Washington University
George Clooney: Northern Kentucky University
Michael Moore: Dropped out first-year University of
 Michigan
Janeane Garafalo: Providence College

"Criticism is prejudice made plausible."

—*H.L. Mencken (1880-1956)*[12]

12 STEPS of the '5 MINUTES OF FAME' PROCESS

Have you ever noticed that people who get their "Five Minutes of Fame" usually experience these same steps?

1. News—Newspapers
2. People Magazine
3. Oprah Winfrey Show
4. Larry King Live
5. Oscar Parties
6. Have plastic surgery
7. Write a Tell-All Book

... then the downhill slide

8. National Enquirer
9. Start your own lingerie, purse, or jewelry collection
10. Pose for Playboy
11. Celebrity Wrestling
12. The Tell-All Book is now at Sam's Club 50% off

IF YOU DON'T LOVE IT, LEAVE IT

How ironic. The word 'sufferage' is a word linked to voting—which coincidentally, bears a likeness to the word *suffer!* Voting is an honor bequeathed by our forefathers who *suffered* and sacrificed greatly in that we may enjoy the process today. What a gift-the freedom to shape our political foundation through the process of elections.

The most unfortunate *suffering* we experience today, seems to be the political wedge that is driving our country further and further apart. In the midst of a country split once again on a pro-war/anti-war stance, split on a republican/democratic platform; one cannot help but wonder if it's the media and entertainment industry fueling this fire of discord throughout our country.

Hey Hollywood . . .

If you don't love it, leave it.

HOLLYWOOD vs. NASHVILLE

Award shows use to be long, boring hours of emotional celebrities rambling on and on thanking a long list of haphazard people you've never even heard of.

Now, award shows are long, boring hours of a few arrogant celebrities stealing the spotlight to air their political views.

At the 2004 Grammy Awards, Coldplay lead singer Chris Martin accepted his award for record of the year. He dedicated his award to Johnny Cash and John Kerry, whom he hopes will be president. Excuse me, but isn't this guy from England? It's bad enough we have our own Americans like Sheryl Crow or Michael Moore using the award shows to sneak in a quick opinion, but now a foreigner too?

Why It's Called 'Country'

Country music artists have proven one of the most patriotic in the music business. Whether it was Clinton or Bush in office, the continuing theme is, has and always will be "God Bless America". At the 2003 Academy of Country Music Awards, Toby Keith sang his powerful anthem *Courtesy of the Red, White and Blue* onstage against a sea of American flags and his acceptance speech included a 'thank you' to our soldiers. What a class act. Aaron Tippin's post September 11th anthem *Where The Stars And Stripes And The Eagle Fly* was equally as patriotic. Charlie Daniels. He is the personification of patriotism and truly captured the magnificence of the American spirit with his music.

Is it West Coast vs. Heartland America? Is it Liberal vs. Conservative? Is it Ego vs. Eagle? Is it No Class vs. Class? How can the entertainment industry, an industry so intertwined, be so totally different? Hollywood exploits award shows for personal politics, whereas country music artists service it as a forum to show love of country ... totally different.

AWARD SHOWS
SHMAWARD SHOWS

I find television very educating. Every time
somebody turns on the set, I go into the other
room and read a book."

Groucho Marx (1890-1977)[13]

I don't mean to harp on celebrities, but man, we sure can get sick of them! On the grocery store tabloids, television shows, talk shows, movies, interviews, magazine articles, The Hollywood Walk of Fame ... stop the madness! I would rather listen to an interview with a postman from Tennessee instead of hearing the latest Paris Hilton antics any day! At least this postman will be *different* and unique and probably share something far more intelligent.

Can you guess how many award shows there are? Twenty, Forty, Sixty? According to a list researched and compiled by Linda Mirabella, editor and publisher of LaStarz, [14] (http://www.lastarz.home) here are the shows listed:

December and January 2003
American Music Awards, Critics Association Awards, Golden Globe Awards, People's Choice Awards, National Board of Review Awards, AFI Awards, DVD Premiere Awards, Golden Satellite Awards, Broadcast Film Critics Association Awards, and more

February 2003
American Cinema Editors Awards, American Society of Cinematographers Awards, Annie Awards, Art directors

Gild Awards, comedy Film Honors, Hollywood Make-up Artists and Hair Stylist Guild Awards, British Academy Film Awards, Grammy Awards, NAACP Image Awards, Rock The Vote Awards, Pioneer Awards, Soul Train Music Awards, Visual Effects Society Awards and more

March 2003
Academy Awards, Chlotrudis Awards, Cinema Audio Society, Costume Designers Awards, Genesis Awards, Golden Reel Awards, Golden Trailer Awards, Independent Spirit Awards, Producers Guild of America, Razzies, Screen Actors Guild Awards, ShoWest Awards, Sports Emmy Awards, TV Land Awards, Writers Gild Awards, and more

April 2003
CMT Flameworthy Video Music Awards, Dove Awards, E's Golden Hanger Awards, Juno Awards, BMI Pop Awards, and more

May 2003
Academy of Country Music Awards, American Federation of Television and Radio Artists, Daytime Emmy Awards, MTV Movie Awards, World Music Awards, and more

June 2003
AFI Life Achievement Awards, ALMA Awards, BET Awards, CFDA Fashion Icon Awards, Essence Awards, TNN Country Music Awards, Tony Awards, Imagen Awards, Saturn Awards,World Stunt Awards, and more

July 2003
ESPY Awards and more

August 2003
Billboard R & B/Hip-Hop Awards, MTV Video Music Awards, Soul Train Lady of Soul Awards, Teen Choice Awards and more

September 2003
Creative Arts Emmy Awards, IFP Gotham Awards, Latin Grammy Awards, Primetime Emmy Awards, and more

October 2003
American choreography Awards, Hollywood Film Awards, MTV Video Music Awards Latin America, VHI-Vogue Fashion Awards and more

November 2003
Country Music Awards, MTV Europe Music Awards and more

December 2003
Billboard Music Awards, European Film Awards, VH-1 Big in 2003 Awards, and more

To top it off, they use sneaky little acronyms so we have no idea what they are awarding. AFI Life Achievement Awards, ALMA Awards, CFDA Fashion Icon Awards . . . what do these stand for? I was so happy they were at least honoring animals at the Dove Awards, until I realized that award has nothing to do with animals! Think of all the animals that have given us years of entertainment; Lassie, Flipper, and Benji . . . no awards for them. Hollywood sure is a dog-eat-dog world.

"Hollywood is a place where they place you
under contract instead of under observation."

—*Walter Winchell (1897-1972)*[15]

O.K. self-indulging entertainment industry! Time to honor us, the people who made you successful.

Here is the list of Award Shows For The Common Man:

JANUARY—SUCKER AWARD
Americans who pay $8/per movie ticket and $10/per popcorn and small drink

FEBRUARY—TABLOID—BENNIFER—AWARD

Proving that reporting the day-by-day relationship between such couples as Ben Affleck and Jennifer Lopez and Jennifer Lopez and Marc Anthony will not make a poignant difference in my life or better our country

MARCH—'NO ONE PROMOTES DONALD TRUMP BETTER THAN DONALD TRUMP' AWARD

Egocentrics hitting the television airwaves at an all-time high. When your boss says 'You're Fired', it's a nightmare. When Donald Trump says 'You're Fired", it's entertainment.

Why don't television execs give Ivana her own show? Instead of "You're Fired", Ivana could say to a group of shocked grooms, "I Just Set Fire To Your Prenuptial Agreement". Now that's entertainment!

APRIL—50 MOST-BEAUTIFUL (BARF) AWARD

Contributing to America's bad reputation as a society obsessed with physical appearance.

Why don't they list the 50 Most Intelligent or the 50 Most Hard-Working?

MAY—REGIS AND KELLY AWARD

Lazy producers refusing to explore new talent and end up picking the same people over and over for different parts. All those hard-working aspiring talent who wait tables by day and go to acting class by night, only to lose a chance at a job because Regis or Kelly already took it!

JUNE—JULY—THE HOORAY FOR ISAAC MIZRAHI TARGET COLLECTION AWARD

Answering the constant wonder of why designers think they can create something that looks like it came out of a garbage dumpster and charge $18,000 because it's got their name on it? Bravo to all the fashion designers who went mainstream. Consumers, rejoice!

AUGUST—LEAVE MEL GIBSON ALONE AWARD
Movie exec's secretly mad because they chose not to finance *The Passion Of The Christ* and will lose a ton of money and respect, the two things Mel Gibson gained as a result

SEPTEMBER "YOU PAID HOW MUCH FOR THOSE TENNIS SHOES?" AWARD
Suckers having to pay for tennis shoes that cost a couple of dollars to make and will retail around $65—most likely to cover the million-dollar endorsements the celebrity/athlete cost the company

OCTOBER—MICHAEL MOORE TREACHERY AWARD
Amazement at how some artists can take their artistic talent and spoil it by shoving their political views so down our throat it makes us throw-up. In other words, hijacking creative talent to be mean-spirited.

NOVEMBER REALITY SERIES CONTESTANTS TORTURE AWARD
Ticking off those same waiters and waitresses going to acting class at night (see May) and are still being overlooked in the entertainment industry for reality-series contestants

DECEMBER—SOAP OPERA-MURPHY'S LAW AWARD
The time-defying technique of how everyone but Susan Lucci from *All My Children* can age and how you can stop watching them for 6 years and your favorite character has already married, divorced, married again, cheated on their spouse, divorced, got in a 'horrible accident', died and came back to life as their twin!

"The human race is faced with a cruel choice:
work or daytime television."

—Author Unknown[16]

CHAPTER 6

One Nation

ENGLISH

Teaching *English as a Second Language* filled my classes
with students from Germany, Saudi Arabia, Argentina, Mexico,
Japan, Taiwan, Korea . . . all over the world. I once asked my
students, "What is the official language of the United States?"

"English"

"English"

"English"

"Spanish" Kid sleeping in my class, I knew it!

"No English is not the official language," I said.

The entire class went into an uproar.

"Oh yes it is Miss Lisa!"

"Oh no it's not!" I retorted.

The class fell silent. I continued.

"The fact is . . . there is no official language of the United
States. Sure, money, tax returns, the Constitution; all aspects
that make up everyday life is in English. But no politician
has taken it upon themselves to make English the *official*
language of the United States."

> "The word 'politics' is derived from the word
> 'poly' meaning 'many' and the word 'ticks'
> meaning 'blood sucking parasites.'"
>
> —*Larry Hardiman*[1]

Politics As Usual.

Did you know in 1988, Arizona made English the official language? Article 28 required all state and local businesses to be conducted in English only. That law was taken to court and challenged by a state insurance claims manager who filed a lawsuit, claiming if she tried to speak to her clients in Spanish, she felt her job would be in jeopardy. The state courts upheld the law, but the federal courts shot it down, on the grounds that it deprived the employee her right to freedom of speech. Ultimately, the case went to the U.S. Supreme Court, who found this case immaterial because the woman was no longer employed by the state of Arizona.

Somehow, in our country's quest to be so darn politically correct, we are doing everything *except* being politically correct! After what happened in Arizona— can't offend so-and-so, can't offend so-and-so, can't offend so-and-so . . . well, you know what Insurance Chick? I'm offended too.

**Do not remove a fly from your friend's forehead
with a hatchet**

—Chinese Proverb[2]

How in the world can Americans assimilate into one society if they can't communicate with each other? How much waste is accumulated in both money and manpower through multi-lingual voting ballots, multi-lingual utility bills and the several other components that linguistically divide our nation? Do you think Uncle Sam is saying, "Aw, don't worry about it. I'll pick up the tab for all that multilingual stuff." No way. He's saying, "Okay ignorant spenders. I take cash, check, credit cards, everything except food stamps because those are mine."

Press 1 for English . . . 2 for Spanish . . . 6 for French . . . 9 for Italian

It is not a question of supremacy. Many people in the world view America as arrogant and feel the wave of English heard 'round the world is American inspired. Yet, according to the US Department of Health, 37 million Americans do not even speak English at home. It's called English . . . not Americanglish . . . so what's all the fuss? Let's go back a couple of centuries and get to the bottom of this.

WHERE IN THE WORLD DID ENGLISH COME FROM?

> "England and America are two countries
> separated by a common language."
>
> *George Bernard Shaw (1856-1950)*[3]

When Britain was part of the Roman Empire, the Romans brought the Latin language to Britain. At that time, the early forms of the English language did not develop mainly from Latin. Only languages such as Spanish and French came directly from Latin. So, basically early English was the language of tribes who invaded from the East. These "tribes" originated from what is known today as Germany. If you speak German, you may have noted that the German and English language have many similarities. The German and English language developed from the same origin and share many of the same words used today.

By 878 AD, the Vikings, who spoke the Norse language, invaded Britain from Scandinavia. The Norse language blended into the old English language that was being spoken at that time. Around 1200, the Kingdoms of England and France separated, and consequently, the use of Old

English came back, but this time many French words were added. This language was known as Middle English.[4] 'Middle English' was very different throughout parts of the country, and since travel was only by foot, horse or ship, sharing information was slow and difficult. But, in 1500 A.D. an invention brought communications out of the Dark Ages— the printing press.[5] The printing press did back then what television and computers have done today; basically skyrocket communication technology into the next level.

Having a common language in print by the 1500's spread Middle English like wildfire, though Latin and Greek were still prevalent across Europe as well. The printing press was an instrumental part of the 'Renaissance' in Europe— a time of great advancement in learning and culture. The 'Renaissance' flourished throughoutEurope with artists such as Leonardo da Vinci and Michaelangelo making great strides in art, whilst William Shakespeare was becoming the most famous playwright in England. His brilliant use of the English language coupled with clever observation of human nature made him, probably the most famous playwright of all time. [6] (sorry Andrew Lloyd Weber (gulp) but, I thought *Cats* was great!)

THE MOST POPULAR BOOK OF ALL TIME

As Shakespeare was celebrated in theatre, a book was printed that would have a significant impact on society and culture; The 'Authorized' or 'King James' translation of the Bible in 1611.[7] Finally, anyone who could read had access to the Bible in their own language. Today, we find this version difficult to understand, but back then, it set a precedent for a unilateral language in print.

Like Shakespeare, the King James Version of the Bible produced many phrases and quotations that have become part of the English language today. People often use these catch phrases without even knowing they come from the King James' translation of the Bible:[8] For example:

> 'turn the other cheek'
> 'go a second mile'
> 'the love of money is the root of all evil'

The English language continued to thrive during the Renaissance. British settlers moved across the world to the United States, Australia, New Zealand, Asia, India and Africa.[9] Throughout the world, English changed and developed, taking in new words from other local languages. For example, 'kangaroo' and 'boomerang' are native Australian Aborigine words. Did you think "ballet" was an English word? Nope. How about 'cappuccino'? Nope.

Even today, English continues to change and develop, with hundreds of new words arriving every year. For example, 'metrosexual' is an adjective for a man who is fixated on his physical appearance and personal style. He is aware of fashion trends and often participates in activities that will enhance his appearance such as manicures, pedicures and facials. Think about it. We never heard Shakespeare say, "Wherefore thou metrosexual man taketh a manicure and pedicure before dusk."

SOME ORIGINS OF WORDS N' PHRASES—

"Honeymoon"

The myth of this word is that it goes back to Babylon, over 4,000 years ago. For one month after the wedding, the bride's father would give his son-in-law an unlimited supply of mead. Mead was a honey beer, and since their lunar calendar was based upon the fermentation of this drink, it was called the 'honey month'. This is where the word 'honeymoon' comes from.

In-laws drinking beer together? No wonder there was no divorce back then! Wait a minute . . . chummy in-laws seems too unusual and needless to say, that theory has since been debunked. Not for the that reason, but more logically because mead is not grown in Babylon, but rather in the northern regions. The word 'honeymoon' actually first appeared around the 16th century. 'Honey' is a reference to the sweetness of a new marriage. 'Moon' is an acknowledgement that this sweetness, will quickly fade, as does a full moon.[10]

Back Then: "Thouest William. I shall marry thee but the depths of my soul realize that this sweetness in our marriage shall fade as does the full moon."

Modern Version: "Hey Billy. You creep. You were so much nicer when we first got hitched. You used to send me flowers. Now, all you do is watch football and go out with the guys."

"Mind Your P's and Q's"

In old English pubs, ale was ordered in the quantity of pints or quarts. When customers got boisterous, the bartender would yell, "Mind your pints and quarts!".[11] Today we hear "mind your p's and q 's", which means pay attention to your behavior.

"Poker"

Our country has gone Poker mad! I even came home from work one day to find my housekeeper glued to the television set, laying on my recliner, watching a poker tournament while my house was collecting dust. I couldn't get mad, for I was up the night before until 3 a.m. doing the exact same thing. With this sudden worldwide addiction to television poker, figure I mind as well find out what the word means.

In America, the game of Poker dates as far back as 1836. Although the origin of the word is uncertain, it may have come from the German verb *pochen*, meaning to brag or to bluff. There is a German card game similar to poker that involves bluffing called *poch*.[12] That makes sense, considering many of our English words come from the German language.

* * *

TRUE OR FALSE?

True or False: English is the most widely spoken language in the world.

Think it's true? Think again. English, with 508 million speakers, is the *second* most widely spoken language.[13] With more than 6 billion people in the world, let's take a look at the top 10 languages of Planet Earth.[14]

1.	Mandarin (Chinese)	over 1 billion
2.	English	508 million
3.	Hindustani	497 million
4.	Spanish	392 million
5.	Russian	277 million
6.	Arabic	246 million
7.	Bengali	211 million (man is India growing!)
8.	Portuguese	191 million
9.	Malay-Indonesian	159 million
10.	French	129 million

Japanese, Korean and Italian didn't make the cut? Population, without a doubt, was the deciding factor in this top ten. Obviously, the most widely spoken languages coincide with the most populous countries. But, Chinese outnumbers English by 2-1. Maybe it just feels like English is the most widely spoken language because the entertainment industry has made such a splash around the world . . . well, . . . maybe not . . . the movie *The Passion of the Christ* is in Aramaic. hmm . . .

SOMETHING TO THINK ABOUT

Another story from my teaching days (sorry), but this one has always tugged at my heartstrings.

One of my students was from the Middle East. We were talking after class and I asked him how he was adjusting to the United States, since he had only arrived the week before. He told me, "I am happy to be here but Teacher, I cannot sleep here in the U.S. It is much quiet. Where I live back home at night there is bombs and explosives each night. There is so much silence in the night here in the U.S. I am not accustomed."

Think about that when you go to sleep tonight . . . and be grateful.

ENGLISH 101 IN 2004

English has unofficially become the world's international language. It has informally become the language of science, air traffic control and most computers. In many countries where several languages are spoken, English is usually the common second language.

"Programming today is a race between software engineers striving to build bigger and better idiot-proof programs, and the Universe trying to produce bigger and better idiots. So far, the Universe is winning."

—*Rich Cook*[15]

Do You Compute?

Some interesting computer language facts:

"There are approximately 172 million English speakers and 163 million non-English speakers online"

(global-reach.biz/globstats)

"50.4% of Web Users speak a native language other than English"

(global-reach.biz/globstats)

"Over 100 million people access the Internet in a language other than English"

(global-reach.biz/globstats)

*   *   *

"Drawing on my fine command of the English language, I said nothing."

Robert Benchley (1889-1945)[16]

STUPID SIGNS

English is a tough language to learn, no doubt. But these silly signs[17] make it evident the English language can be just plain crazy!

Outside a pawn shop:
WE EXCHANGE ANYTHING—BICYCLES, WASHING MACHINES, ETC. WHY NOT BRING YOUR WIFE ALONG AND GET A WONDERFUL BARGAIN?

Notice in health food shop window:
CLOSED DUE TO ILLNESS

Spotted in a safari park:
ELEPHANTS PLEASE STAY IN YOUR CAR

Message on a leaflet:
IF YOU CANNOT READ, THIS LEAFLET WILL TELL
YOU HOW TO GET LESSONS

On a repair shop door:
WE CAN REPAIR ANYTHING. (PLEASE KNOCK HARD
ON THE DOOR—THE BELL DOESN'T WORK)

*   *   *

WHY ENGLISH IS SO HARD TO LEARN

You can *make up* a story or put on *make up*
Put on make up or *put off* what you postpone
Don't drive in *traphic* or buy what you can't *aphord*
Oops, spelling changes when 'f' sounds in words like
    elephant or *phone*

You don't have to *go out* to *figure out* a problem
Look up at the sky, but *look up* information in a book
Shake it today or yesterday *shook*
Take it today or past tense *took*

You can *see* it now or *saw* it when you were away,
But you can't *feel* it now and *faw* it yesterday
What kind of asks specific information, like 'What kind of
    fruit do you eat?
But just *kind of* means 'sort of' 'a little' that *kind of* thing

When you *keep* something, it means to 'hold it' 'save it' or 'store'
But *hold it* means 'halt' 'wait a minute' 'move no more'
Keep on means 'don't stop' encouraging go on a little more
Keep out means 'don't come in' usually a sign on a kids' door

You can travel by taxi, by subway or send information by fax
You can also by mistake, pay *by* check, but please pay *in* cash
With is used for parts of the body or instruments
With a key, not *by* a key, is the best way to say this

Turn up the volume, but there's a vegetable called a 'turnip'
Let us be friends, remember the other vegetable called
    'lettuce'?
If you're talking about yesterday it was *told us* and *sold us*
If it's today, you should say *tell us* and *sell us*

I *used to* live in New York
But now I'm getting *used to* living in Chicago
I'm *accustomed* to Chicago, the people, the town
Is it a *custom* to tell people I've lived all around?

Close the door or *hang up* those *clothes* on the floor!
Hang up the telephone, or even have a few *hang—ups*
    yourself
I think you are getting *close*, it's getting easier to understand,
Probably easiest to learn when *hanging out* with some friends

When you *consider* you're 'thinking about' . . . "I'm consid-
ering going to the lake and fish"
When you are *considerate* you are thoughtful, caring and
    unselfish
Call off means to cancel but *shut off* is the same as *turn off*,
    something that must end
Are you *turned off* by all of this, which means to be disgusted?

This is *too* complicated for the *two* of us *to* understand.

Is it to, two or too, I can't seem *to* comprehend
I want to figure it out *too*, but I'm just *too* lazy
Or maybe it's true . . . the English language is just plain crazy!

**Press 31 for Russian . . . Press 186 for Swahili . . .
Press 267 to hear the choices again . . . Press
3485426 if this irritates you . . .**

CHAPTER 7

UNDER GOD

"Those people who will not be governed by
God will be ruled by tyrants."

—*William Penn*[1]

WRITTEN BY A PASTOR AND
HE LEFT GOD OUT?

*T*he *Pledge of Allegiance* was written by a Baptist minister named Frances Bellamy in 1892 and all references to religion were deliberately left out. Published in Boston, Massachusetts, *The Pledge of Allegiance* was part of the festivities celebrating the 400th Anniversary of the discovery of America.[2]

The phrase "Under God" was later added to the *Pledge* by Congressional approval in an Act passed on June 14, 1954. The words "under God" were inserted at the height of paranoia about the "godless communists". At that time, President Eisenhower said, "In this way we are reaffirming the transcendence of religious faith in America's heritage and future; in this way we shall constantly strengthen those spiritual weapons which forever will be our country's most powerful resource in peace and war."[3]

In layman's 2004 terms, President Eisenhower probably meant this.

*Hey Jack. We're fighting communism and we need
God on our side. You don't have to believe in God, but
our founding father's did believe and they acknowl-
edged Him while setting up this great nation. You
don't HAVE to believe in God, go believe in whatever
you want—we'll give you freedom of religion. But you
do have to respect the fact that our country well-
regards this religious principle.*

"The government of the United States is not, in
any sense, founded on the Christian religion."

—*George Washington (1732-1799)*[4]

This statement by George Washington is proof our
founding fathers were not holy roller—religious-freaks
when they set up our new country.

God was merely venerated . . . period.

NINTH CIRCUIT COURT OF APPEALS or is it the NINTH *CIRCUS* COURT OF *APPALL*?

I didn't believe an ounce of Sigmund Freud's theories
when I studied psychology, but, wouldn't it be ridiculous
to hire a lawyer and sue my high school teacher for
teaching The Oedipus Complex?

I'm sure you remember hearing the story about an atheist
in California that did not want his child to recite the *Pledge of
Allegiance* in school because of the words "under God". The
case went to the Ninth Circuit Court of Appeals who ruled
that the words, "under God" in the *Pledge* as unconstitutional.

Following that decision, in separate resolutions, both
the Senate and the House urged legal action to appeal the
U.S. Ninth Circuit Court of Appeals decision. An appeal

for an en banc hearing before the full appellate court was turned down by the Ninth Circuit. The Ninth Circuit Court of Appeals found the insertion of the religious statement a violation of the Establishment Clause. In a separate motion, on March 3, an amendment to the Constitution was introduced in the Senate that would allow the addition of "under God" to the *Pledge*.

This case went all the way to the Supreme Court. In June of 2004, The Supreme Court ruled in favor of keeping 'under God' in *The Pledge of Allegiance* for now. The Court claimed since the divorced man was in the process of a custody-battle for his child, he was not the legal guardian and therefore, could not legally speak for the child.

What a coincidence. The English Speaking Arizona Case was null-and-void because the woman no longer worked for the company. The atheist man case was null-and-void because the father was not the legal guardian of the child. Amazing how our court system managed to skirt the issue and *twice* ignore the huge elephant in the living room. What a mess . . . what a waste . . . of taxpayer dollars.

MORE WASTE OF TAXPAYER DOLLARS

California . . . again. Plagued with earthquakes, mudslides, forest fires, Anna Nicole Smith, smog and other disasters; this is one state that *needs* a higher-power on their side. I wonder if that's why they elected Arnold *The Terminator* Schwarzenegger Governor? Californians, hate to break it to you . . . but it's just a movie. The way you keep taking God out of everything, you are going to need more than God and *The Terminator* on your side.

In June of 2004, the ACLU ordered the city of Los Angeles to take the crosses (that you practically need a microscope to see) out of the Los Angeles County seal. The large pagan goddess Pomona in the middle of the seal was fine, but they were disturbed by the tiny crosses located on the right side of the seal. The ACLU completely ignored the fact that those crosses are a symbol historically, not religiously in paying homage to early missionary settlers. It is estimated it will cost their already bankrupt state in the multi-millions of dollars. Think about it; flags, stationary, hospitals, jails, county offices, monuments; that seal is everywhere.

If California were smart, they would make the group of people who are against the cross *and* the ACLU foot the enormous bill, instead of the taxpayers of California. Their own money? I wonder how many of them would be complaining then.

What's next, rename Los Angeles, Santa Barbara, Santa Monica, San Francisco, San Diego and every other 'touch' of religious undertone throughout the state? I'm scared the next time I exclaim, "Oh my God" someone from the ACLU is going to jump out of the bushes and attack me with a lawsuit.

Instead of representing civil rights, one of the ACLU's secret agendas appears to be to slowly erase religion out of every aspect of our country's history . . . and let taxpayers pick up the tab. They are not representing my civil liberties when they do that. Equality? I don't think so.

ACLU—CIVIL RIGHTS ORGANIZATION OR TOTALITARIANISM AT ITS FINEST?

The ACLU, or the American Civil Liberties Union, began as a credible organization.Their website claims: The ACLU is our nation's guardian of liberty. We work daily in courts, legislatures and communities to defend and preserve the individual rights and liberties guaranteed to every person in this country by the Constitution and laws of the United States.Our job is to conserve America's original civic values-the Constitution and the Bill of Rights.[5]

What may have started as a no government funding-watchdog group, has evolved into an organization that does not defend or conserve the original civic values of the Constitution and the Bill of Rights, but rather manipulates them to fill the needs of their particular agenda.Again, they never defended my right to protect the history of our country . . . and those little crosses on the Los Angeles County *is* a symbol of California's history. It is wrong to try and erase history to meet personal schema.

Personal Note To ACLU:

I must confess. When I contacted the ACLU, the New York office was incredibly accommodating and everyone I spoke to was extremely helpful. It was then, I realized there were kind human-beings attached to the organization I had critiqued. So, ACLU, it's the agendas I am opposing, not the people or the organization as a whole.

MAJORITY RULES?

In all this Anti-God hysteria, I wondered the religious breakdown of both our country and the world. After examining the breakdowns, it is evident God is not the majority worldwide. But here at home I wonder how the anti-God voices are heard so much louder than the pro-God voices?

RELIGIONS OF THE WORLD[6]

19.6%	Muslims
13.31%	Hindus
12.83%	Other Religions
12.53%	Non Religious
5.88%	Buddhists
5.62%	Protestants
3.51%	Orthodox
2.44%	Atheists
1.31%	Anglicans
.38%	Sikhs
.24%	Jews

RELIGIONS OF THE UNITED STATES

56%   Protestant
28%   Roman Catholic
10%   None
4 %   Other
2 %   Jewish

Majority rules? I don't think so. It's more like the squeaky wheel gets the oil.

ALL 50 STATES MESSED UP?

Since the Ninth Circuit Court of Appeals pushed the envelope on this subject, I can't help but wonder why the judge didn't do his homework, especially in his home state of California.

All 50 states acknowledge God in their state constitutions:

Alabama 1901, Preamble. We the people of the State of Alabama, invoking the favor and guidance of Almighty God, do ordain and establish the following Constitution . . . Alaska 1956, Preamble. We, the people of Alaska, grateful to God and to those who founded our nation and pioneered this great land

. . .

Arizona 1911, Preamble. We, the people of the State of Arizona, grateful to Almighty God for our liberties, do ordain this Constitution . . .

. . .

Arkansas 1874, Preamble. We, the people of the State of Arkansas, grateful to Almighty God for the privilege of choosing our own form of government . . .

. . .

California 1879, Preamble. We, the People of the State of California, grateful to Almighty God for our freedom.

. . .

Colorado 1876, Preamble. We, the people of Colorado, with profound reverence for the Supreme Ruler of Universe.

. . .

Connecticut 1818, Preamble. The People of Connecticut, acknowledging with gratitude the good Providence of God in permitting them to enjoy

. . .

Delaware 1897, Preamble. Through Divine Goodness all men have, by nature, the rights ofworshiping and serving their Creator according to the dictates of their consciences

. . .

Florida 1885, Preamble. We, the people of the State of Florida, grateful to Almighty God for our constitutional liberty . . . establish this Constitution . . .

. . .

Georgia 1777, Preamble. We, the people of Georgia, relying upon protection and guidance of Almighty God, do ordain and establish this Constitution . . .

. . .

Hawaii 1959, Preamble. We, the people of Hawaii, Grateful for Divine Guidance . . . establish this Constitution.

. . .

Idaho 1889, Preamble. We, the people of t! he State of Idaho, grateful to Almighty God for our freedom, to secure its blessings

. . .

Illinois 1870, Preamble. We, the people of the State of Illinois, grateful to Almighty God for the civil, political and religious liberty which He hath so long permitted us to enjoy and looking to Him for a blessing on our endeavors.

. . .

Indiana 1851, Preamble. We, the People of the State of Indiana, grateful to Almighty God for the free exercise of the right to chose our form of government.

. . .

Iowa 1857, Preamble. We, the People of the State of Iowa, grateful to the Supreme Being for the blessings hitherto enjoyed, and feeling our dependence on Him for a continuation of these blessings establish this Constitution

. . .

Kansas 1859, Preamble. We, the people of Kansas, grateful to Almighty God for our civil and religious privileges . . . establish this Constitution.

. . .

Kentucky 1891, Preamble. We, the people of the Commonwealth of grateful to Almighty God for the civil, political and religious liberties . . .

. . .

Louisiana 1921, Preamble. We, the people of the State of Louisiana, grateful to Almighty God for the civil, political and religious liberties we enjoy.

. . .

Maine 1820, Preamble. We the People of Maine . . . acknowledging with grateful hearts the goodness of the

Sovereign Ruler of the Universe in affording us an opportunity and imploring His aid and direction.

. . .

Maryland 1776, Preamble. We, the people of the state of Maryland, grateful to Almighty God or our civil and religious liberty . . .

. . .

Massachusetts 1780, Preamble. We . . . the people of Massachusetts, acknowledging with grateful hearts, the goodness of the Great Legislator of the Universe in the course of His Providence, an opportunity and devoutly imploring His direction

. . .

Michigan 1908, Preamble. We, the people of the State of Michigan, grateful to Almighty God for the blessings of freedom . . . establish this Constitution

. . .

Minnesota 1857, Preamble. We, the people of the State of Minnesota, grateful to God for our civil and religious liberty, and desiring to perpetuate its blessings.

. . .

Mississippi 1890, Preamble. We, the people of Mississippi in convention assembled, grateful to Almighty God, and invoking His blessing on our work.

. . .

Missouri 1845, Preamble. We, the people of Missouri, with profound reverence for the Supreme Ruler of the Universe, and grateful for His goodness establish this Constitution

. . .

Montana 1889, Preamble. We, the people of Montana, grateful to Almighty God for the blessings of liberty. establish this Constitution

. . .

Nebraska 1875, Preamble. We, the people, grateful to Almighty God for our freedom . . . establish this Constitution.

. . .

Nevada 1864, Preamble. We the people of the State of Nevada, grateful to Almighty God for our freedom establish this Constitution

. . .

New Hampshire 1792, Part I. Art. I. Sec. V. Every individual has a natural and unalienable right to worship God according to the dictates of his own conscience.

. . .

New Jersey 1844, Preamble. We, the people of the State of New Jersey, grateful to Almighty God for civil and religious liberty which He hath so long permitted us to enjoy, and looking to Him for a blessing on our endeavors

. . .

New Mexico 1911, Preamble. We, the People of New Mexico, grateful to Almighty God for the blessings of liberty

. . .

New York 1846, Preamble. We, the people of the State of New York, grateful to Almighty God for our freedom, in order to secure its blessings.

. . .

North Carolina 1868, Preamble. We the people of the State of North Carolina, grateful to Almighty God, the Sovereign

Ruler of Nations, for our civil, political, and religious liberties, and acknowledging our dependence upon Him for the continuance of those North Dakota 1889, Preamble. We, the people of North Dakota, grateful to Almighty God for the blessings of civil and religious liberty, do ordain

. . .

Ohio 1852, Preamble. We the people of the state of Ohio, grateful to Almighty God for our freedom, to secure its blessings and to promote our common

. . .

Oklahoma 1907, Preamble. Invoking the guidance of Almighty God, in order to secure and perpetuate the blessings of liberty establish this

. . .

Oregon 1857, Bill of Rights, Article I. Section 2. All men shall be secure in the Natural right, to worship Almighty God according to the dictates of their consciences

. . .

Pennsylvania 1776, Preamble. We, the people of Pennsylvania, grateful to Almighty God for the blessings of civil and religious liberty, and humble invoking His guidance.

. . .

Rhode Island 1842, Preamble. We the People of the State of Rhode Island grateful to Almighty God for the civil and religious liberty which He hath so long permitted us to enjoy, and looking to Him for a blessing

. . .

South Carolina, 1778, Preamble. We, the people of he State of South Carolina, grateful to God for our liberties, do ordain and establish this Constitution.

. . .

South Dakota 1889, Preamble. We, the people of South Dakota, grateful to Almighty God for our civil! and religious liberties establish this

. . .

Tennessee 1796, Art. XI.III. That all men have a natural and indefeasible right to worship Almighty God according to the dictates of their conscience

. . .

Texas 1845, Preamble. We the People of the Republic of Texas, acknowledging, with gratitude, the grace and beneficence of God.

. . .

Utah 1896, Preamble. Grateful to Almighty God for life and liberty, we establish this Constitution.

. . .

Vermont 1777, Preamble. Whereas all government ought to . . . enable the individuals who compose it to enjoy their natural rights, and other blessings which the Author of Existence has bestowed on man

. . .

Virginia 1776, Bill of Rights, XVI . . . Religion, or the Duty which we owe our Creator can be directed only by Reason and that it is the mutual duty of all to practice Christian Forbearance, Love and Charity towards each other

. . .

Washington 1889, Preamble. We the People of the State of Washington, grateful! to the Supreme Ruler of the Universe for our liberties do ordain this Constitution

. . .

West Virginia 1872, Preamble. Since through Divine Providence we enjoy the blessings of civil, political and religious liberty, we, the people of West Virginia . . . reaffirm our faith in and constant reliance upon God . . .

. . .

Wisconsin 1848, Preamble. We, the people of Wisconsin, grateful to Almighty God for our freedom, domestic tranquility . . .

. . .

Wyoming 1890, Preamble. We, the people of the State of Wyoming, grateful to God for our civil, political, and religious liberties establish this Constitution

Colorado named God *The Supreme Ruler of Universe* and Maine referred to Him as the *Sovereign Ruler of the Universe* . . . either way, God clearly is the prominent core in the early historical text of this country. From our money *In God We Trust* to the swearing in at a court of law with *the whole truth and nothing but the truth, so help me God*, God is the significant dynamic that fashioned the founding of our nation.

Too bad God is not on our tax returns—sure need a 'higher power' in *that* department! Since 1776 (228 years . . . wow!) America has been acknowledging God.

If it ain't broke, don't fix it.

*   *   *

. . . if there is not a God . . . who pops-up the next tissue out of the box?

UNDERSTANDING THE ATHIESTS

"I once wanted to become an atheist, but I gave
up—they have no holidays."

—*Henny Youngman (1906-1998)*[7]

First off, as Americans we must respect all religious and non-religious views. It's called *Freedom of Religion*. Period. This does not include *freedom-of-religion-but-I-wanna-change-everything-our-founding-fathers-started-to-fit-my-personal-philosophy*.

As a believer in God, I felt the need to understand the man in California and his point of view. Though no two atheists think alike, I found a reasonable explanation in the world of Philosophy with the help of the concepts of Possibilism and Actualism.[8]

In Metaphysics, there are two dividing forces-Possibilism and Actualism. Possibilism implies that something may or may not exist, whereas Actualism exists in fact or reality. Although this concept dates back to the 14th century, it is similar to modern-day forces such as good and bad, black and white and ying and yang. All forces must have an action and reaction. These two forces are neither "correct" nor "incorrect", but rather provide an opposing force in personal philosophy.

Our founding fathers had the typical characteristics of a Possibilist. As Possibilists, they dared to dream and saw a possibility. Nature, manners or customs were decided through a "belief". There was no need for facts or statistics. As religion dictates, there is God, as well as intangible objects such as "faith" and "love". Possiblists feel ideals such as God, faith and love are indeed a reality, though there is no physical proof.

Atheists are not "bad people" or "anti-God". They merely live their life with the philosophy bearing the burden of proof. I think we are all born "Possibilists" but somehow the Possibilist child dies and the Actualist teenager is born. Maybe it's when we find out there is no Santa Claus, discover wrestling on television is fake or that Uncle Bob wears a toupee, who knows. But, as we grow older, we develop a need for statistics, numbers, and facts. In other words, the harsh voice of reality. As intelligent creatures, humans have the innate quest to acquire knowledge. Actualists must have concrete proof and cannot believe something they cannot "see".

When people read their horoscope in the newspaper, most accept the reasoning in astrology and horoscopes. The history of the horoscope dates back to ancient civilization, for ancient astrologers used the logic of cosmic placement as factual explanation. Stellar and constellation alignment is the scientific "proof" that validates astrology to many people.

Horoscopes and Religion are similar in their development. Just as stars and the universe connect with people looking for answers, the concept of God connects with people looking for answers as well. But, does God really exist? What came first, the chicken or the egg? Modern Day version: Who came first, Britney Spears or Christina Aguilera? Christians consider the egg as a symbol of life, but it doesn't mean that it is the answer. There are many possible ways for Christians to live and think, but their belief in Jesus and his appearance on Earth justified the concept of the One God. Jesus was the "proof' they needed. But, it doesn't mean it was "proof" for everyone in the world. The Jewish people are still waiting for their messiah, or their "proof' that their God exists.

Religion is a process. Humans create religions, and religions create humans. First, humans decide their values, then they institutionalize them. Religions are the institutions that preserve these values. Institutions also represent the humans who created them and humans represent the institutions they created. Religion, like culture and society, are human creations. Next time you pass a Methodist church, do not consider it a 'building', but rather a creation of those who believe in its values.

Actualists, like Atheists, need that "concrete proof" and live their life accordingly. Though I respect the philosophy of the man in California, he in turn must respect the philosophy by which our nation was founded.

But, amongst all this philosophical mish-mash . . . the question still lies.

Who came first? Britney Spears or Christina Aguilera?

*   *   *

"The worst moment for the atheist is when he is really thankful and has nobody to thank."

Dante Gabriel Rossetti (1828-1882)[9]

*   *   *

GOD 'SIGHTINGS' AROUND THE COUNTRY

"What can you say about a society that says that God is dead and Elvis is alive?"

—*Irv Kupcinet*[10]

The Washington Monument

Construction began for this giant obelisk in 1848 under President James Polk. It was opened to the public in 1888. Atop the monument are engraved words, measuring 555 feet high, which read LAUS DEO, meaning 'Praise Be To God'.[11]

The $1 Bill

Next time you happen to be studying the back of a $1 bill, notice the seal with a pyramid, a large eye and two Latin phrases.

The pyramid is a symbol of *strength* and *durability*. It is an unfinished pyramid, indicating our country will always grow, improve and build.

The large eye located above the pyramid suggests the *importance of divine guidance in favor of the American cause.*

NOVUS ORDO SECLORUM translates as *A New Order of the Ages* signifying the new American era.

ANNUIT COEPTIS means *He (God) has favored our undertakings.*[12]

Do you think God is favoring how we are taking Him out of all our undertakings now?

*   *   *

I'm still an atheist, Thank God."

Luis Bunuel (1900-1983)[13]

CHAPTER 8

INDIVISIBLE

"In the truest sense, freedom cannot be bestowed; it must be achieved."

—*Franklin D. Roosevelt in a speech on September 22, 1936[1]*

September 11, 2001 is undoubtedly the darkest hour in modern American history. We lost thousands of lives on our own soil. Yet, we Americans have a short memory. Americans were horrified on September 11th, but what about the other horrific events that have plagued our countrymen?

1. The bombing of the U.S.S. Cole
2. The bombing of the World Trade Center in 1993
3. The bombing of the American Consulate in South Africa

"Let him who desires peace prepare for war."

—*Flavius Vegetius Renatus (375 AD) De Rei Militari[2]*

ATTACKS ON AMERICA

War did not begin September 11, 2001 or even March 19, 2002. According to the Center for Arms Control and

Non-Proliferation[3] these are ONLY A FEW listings of terrorist acts against the United States.

1979

November 4
Iranian radicals seize the US Embassy in Tehran, taking sixty-six American diplomats hostage. The crisis continues until January 20, 1981 when the hostages are released by diplomatic means.

1983

April 18
Sixty three people, including the CIA's Middle East Director, are killed and 120 injured in a suicide truck bomb attack on the US Embassy in Beirut, Lebanon. Responsibility is claimed by Islamic Jihad.

October 23
Simultaneous suicide truck bombs on American and French compounds in Beirut, Lebanon. A 12,000 lb bomb destroys a US Marine Corps base killing two hundred and forty one Americans; another fifty eight Frenchmen are killed when a 400 lb device destroys one of their bases. Islamic Jihad claims responsibility.

December 12

US Embassy in Kuwait targeted by Iraqi Shia terrorists who attempted to destroy the building with a truck bomb. The attack was foiled by guards and the device exploded in the Embassy fore-court killing five people.

1984

March 16
CIA station chief in Beirut, Lebanon, William Buckley, was kidnapped by the Iranian backed Islamic Jihad. He was tortured and then executed by his captors.

September 20
Suicide bomb attack on US Embassy in East Beirut kills twenty three people and injures twenty one others. The US and British ambassadors were slightly injured in the explosion which was attributed to the Iranian backed Hezbollah group.

1985

June 14
A Trans World Airlines flight was hijacked en route to Rome from Athens by two Lebanese Hezbollah terrorists and forced to fly to Beirut. The eight crew members and 145 passengers were held for 17 days, during which one American hostage, a U.S. Navy diver, was murdered. After being flown twice to Algiers, the aircraft was returned to Beirut after Israel released 435 Lebanese and Palestinian prisoners.

October 7
Four Palestinian Liberation Front terrorists seized an Italian cruise liner in the eastern Mediterranean Sea, taking more than 700 hostages. One U.S. passenger was murdered before the Egyptian Government offered the terrorists safe haven in return for the hostages' freedom.

October 21
American businessman Edward Tracy kidnapped in
Lebanon by Islamic terrorists and held for almost five years
until August 11, 1991.

1986

March 30
A Palestinian splinter group detonated a bomb as TWA Flight
840 approached Athens Airport, killing four U.S. citizens.

April 5
Two U.S. soldiers were killed, and 79 American servicemen
were injured in a Libyan bomb attack on a nightclub in
West Berlin, West Germany.

1987

January 24th
American citizens Jesse Turner and Alann Steen w were seized
in Beirut by Islanmic terrorists. Turner was held until October
22, 1991 and Steen was released on December 3, 1991.

April 24
Sixteen U.S. servicemen riding in a Greek Air Force bus near
Athens were injured in an apparent bombing attack, carried
out by the revolutionary organization known as 17 November.

1988

February 17
US Marine Corps Lieutenant Colonel W. Higgens,
kidnapped and murdered by the Iranian backed Hezbollah
while serving with the United Nations Truce Supervisory
Organization in southern Lebanon.

April 14
The Organization of Jihad Brigades exploded a car bomb outside a USO Club in Naples, Italy, killing one U.S. sailor.

June 28
US Naval Attache killed in Athens, Greece, by November 17th terrorist group

August 8
Pakistan president Zia Al Haq and US ambassador are killed, along with thirty seven other people, when a bomb explodes on a C-130 Hercules aircraft just after take off from Bahawalpu, Pakistan.

December 21
Pan Am Boeing 747 blown up over Lockerbie, Scotland, by a bomb believed to have been placed on the aircraft at Frankfurt Airport, Germany. All 259 people on the aircraft were killed by the blast.

1993

February 26
World Trade Center in New York, USA, attacked by a massive bomb planted by Islamic terrorists.

April 14th
Iraqi intelligence service attempt to assassinate former US President, George Bush, during a visit to Kuwait.

1995

March 8
Two unidentified gunmen killed two U.S. diplomats and wounded a third in Karachi, Pakistan.

August 21
Hamas claimed responsibility for the detonation of a bomb in Jerusalem that killed six and injured over 100 persons, including several U.S. citizens.

November 13
Seven foreigners, including a number of US servicemen, are killed in bomb attack on National Guard training centre at Riyadh, Saudi Arabia.

1996

June 25
Islamic radical terrorists opposed to the western military presence in the Gulf region, explode a truck bomb next to a USAF housing area at Dhahran, Saudi Arabia, killing 19 American servicemen and 385 injuring more.

1997

February 23
A Palestinian gunman opened fire on tourists at an observation deck atop the Empire State Building in New York City, killing a Danish national and wounding visitors from the United States, Argentina, Switzerland, and France before turning the gun on himself. A handwritten note carried by the gunman claimed this was a punishment attack against the "enemies of Palestine."

November 12
Two unidentified gunmen shot to death four U.S. auditors from Union Texas Petroleum Corporation and their Pakistani driver after they drove away from the Sheraton Hotel in Karachi. The Islami Inqilabi Council, or Islamic

Revolutionary Council, claimed responsibility in a call to the U.S. Consulate in Karachi. In a letter to Pakistani newspapers, the Aimal Khufia Action Committee also claimed responsibility.

1998

August 7
US Embassies in Nairobi, Kenya, and Dar-es-Salem, Tanzania, heavily damaged by massive bomb attacks. US intelligence blames Islamic groups linked to Saudi dissident Osama Bin Laden.

December 28
Yemini militants kidnap a group of western tourists, including 12 Britons, 2 Americans, and 2 Australians on the main road to Aden. Four victims were killed during a rescue attempt the next day.

2000

August 12
In the Kara-Su Valley, the Islamic Movement of Uzbekistan took four U.S. citizens hostage. The Americans escaped on August 12.

October 12
In Aden, Yemen, a small dingy carrying explosives rammed the destroyer U.S.S. Cole, killing 17 sailors and injuring 39 others. Supporters of Usama Bin Ladin were suspected.

December 30
A bomb exploded in a plaza across the street from the U.S. embassy in Manila, injuring nine persons. The Moro Islamic Liberation Front is allegedly responsible.

2001

September 11
The date says it all.
Two hijacked airliners crashed into the twin towers of the World Trade Center. Soon thereafter, the Pentagon was struck by a third hijacked plane. A fourth hijacked plane, suspected to be bound for a high-profile target in Washington, crashed into a field in southern Pennsylvania. More than 3,000 U.S. citizens and other nationals were killed. President Bush and Cabinet officials indicated that Usama Bin Laden was the prime suspect and that they considered the United States in a state of war with international terrorism.

Injustice anywhere is a threat to justice everywhere."

—*Martin Luther King Jr. (1929-1968)*[4]

WAR/NO-WAR/WAR/NO-WAR

WHEW! Not enough for you? That was only a *partial* list. War is too complicated and too controversial to make a stance. So, let's look at both sides:

#1. President Bush came under fire for his decision (and Legislative approval for the use of force, don't forget) in choosing war. But, if you were a mother who lost your child in the bombing of the U.S.S. Cole in Yemen, how would you feel about the more pacifist stance President Clinton took? Remember, September 11th stunned us to the point that we did not know who or where the enemy lay. And here we are, still in a war where we do not know who or where the enemy lay. War is a tough topic . . . an old

Spanish Proverb says *Never advise anyone to go to war or to marry*. But, at the same time, should those who died in the terrorist acts listed die in vain?

#2. Many feel America has its' fingers in too many foreign pies. The anti-war stance is coupled with 'Why don't we just leave other countries alone!" Many felt we should not have overthrown a dictatorship without the world's approval, and ultimately, finding that our intelligence was flawed.

Flashback

Imagine This Scenario: Suppose Canada invades England. England asks for our help.We hesitate and hesitate, thinking, "Wait. Canada is our neighbor. We do a lot of business with Canada. We have a lot of government contracts with Canada. Do we really want to get involved?" My guess is, something like that was happening when so many countries were hesitant to fight the War on Terror. No country wants to bite the hand that feeds them.

Although Iraq was granted sovereignty on June 28, 2004, this War on Terror is more horrific than the world surmises, fighting an enemy no one can see. Terror has gone on for decades and judging from the world news, it is far from over and involves, not just America, but the entire world. No one on earth is free from this terror. The bombing in Madrid . . . the bombing in Bali . . . the school tragedy in Beslan.

Whether you are for or against the war, the most important thing to remember is that it is imperative to support the men and women in uniform, who are merely fulfilling their duty that comes with an incredibly dangerous job.

SENATOR GLENN "Moons"
SENATOR METZENBAUM

Senator Glenn rose to the occasion and spoke for so many who have served our country well.The following excerpt is between Senators John Glenn and Sen. Howard Metzenbaum: Senator Metzenbaum to Senator Glenn:[5]

"How can you run for Senate when you've never held a "real job"?

Senator Glenn:

"I served 23 years in the United States Marine Corps. I served through two wars. I flew 149 missions. My plane was hit by anti-aircraft fire on 12 different occasions. I was in the Space Program. It wasn't my checkbook, Howard; it was my Life on the line.It was not a nine to five job, where I took time off to take the daily cash receipts to the bank. I ask you to go with me . . . as I went the other day . . . to a Veterans Hospital and look those men—with their mangled bodies—in the eye, andtell THEM they didn't hold a job! You go with me to the Space Program at NASA and go, as I have gone, to the widows and orphans of Ed White, Gus Grissom and Roger Chaffee and you look those kids in the eye and tell them that their Dad's didn't hold a job. You go with me on Memorial Day and you stand in Arlington National Cemetery, where I have more friends buried than I'd like to remember,and you watch those waving flags. You stand there, and you think about this Nation,and you tell ME that those people didn't have a job? I'll tell you,Howard Metzenbaum, you should be on your knees every day of your lifethanking God that there were some men—SOME MEN—who held a REAL job.And they required a dedication to a purpose— and a love of country anda dedication to duty—that was more important than life itself. Andtheir self-sacrifice is what made this country possible. I HAVE held a job, Howard!—What about you?

NO BROTHERHOOD IN THE HOOD

"The universal brotherhood of man is our most
precious possession."

—*Mark Twain 1835-1910*[6]

In this excerpt from *America The Beautiful*, notice the
reference to 'brotherhood'

America The Beautiful

Katharine Lee Bates (1859-1929)[7]

Oh beautiful for spacious skies
For amber waves of grain
For purple mountain majesties . . .
America! America!
God shed his grace on thee,
And crown thy good with brotherhood
From sea to shining sea.

Katharine Lee Bates was an instructor at Wellesley
College when she wrote that in 1893. It was written after a
trip to Colorado, where she climbed Pikes Peak and got
inspired.[8] Back then, her poem rang of "brotherhood" from
sea to shining sea. Forget sea to shining sea, I can't find any
brotherhood from legislator to shining legislator!

TRUST, BOYFRIENDS AND LEGISLATORS

I once dated a guy who broke up with me because he
said, "I can't date a girl who doesn't trust me." Let's take a
look at the big picture.

When we started dating exclusively, he informed me that in two months he was going to Las Vegas on a trip with his ex-girlfriend. At first, he said it was a 'business trip', but a few minutes later, admitted the trip was *really* scheduled when they were dating and it came about because she happened to have that particular time off from work and they were still very good friends.

Okay. I am supposed to trust a guy who says I cannot go to lunch with another man, states we should date exclusively, but in two months he's going on a trip with his ex-girlfriend to (not a church-related retreat in Idaho) but Las "glitter gulch" Vegas? Trust? Was he joking?

In retrospect, he sure would have made a great politician! "Hey trust me. I do things that are completely selfish. None of my actions have proved me worthy of trust. But hey! Trust me!" *Hard to tell if that was a sleazy boyfriend or a sleazy politician talking, huh? Scary.*

So many politicians seem to have the reputation of being untrustworthy, but it is their actions that have gotten them such a bad rap. Politicians just assume we should trust them . . . boom . . . that's it. Trust is *earned* over time through actions. And, when you have someone's trust, you ultimately have their respect.

I hope politicians realize via this little story, that trust and respect of the American public can only be *earned*.

TWO-FACED POLITICIANS

America was truly moved when lawmakers gathered on the Capitol steps to sing patriotic songs on September 11th. It was a beautiful witnessing to the 'brotherhood' Katharine Lee Bates wrote about. What a shame it took a national tragedy, for our lawmakers to put aside bi-partisan agendas and unite as one country.

Well guys and gals on Capitol Hill, we haven't seen much of that "brotherhood" since. All that fighting and mudslinging for your personal agendas . . . yuck, that's why it's called "mud"slinging . . . it's dirty and nasty and gross. All in all, I can't figure out what you democrats and republicans care more about—strengthening my country or strengthening your own political platforms.

> "Government is too big and too important to be
> left to the politicians."
>
> —*Chester Bowles (1901-1986)* [9]

UNSOCIAL SOCIAL SECURITY

Legislators may argue, "What's the big deal? We haven't done anything wrong." Oh contraire.

I never understood why Legislators rant and rave about the state of Social Security, but they never do anything about it. Do you know why they could care less? The indifference is because Senators and Congressmen do not pay into Social Security. True, they do not collect on it either, but, why should they? They don't need Social Security since they passed into law their own retirement plan. The Golden Fleece Retirement Plan. How appropriate that the plan has the word "fleece" in it since that is exactly what they are doing with *our* money! Money that comes out of the 'General Fund'. What exactly is the 'General Fund'? I researched and found nothing, so I invented my own definition.

Unofficial Definition of General Fund
noun

1. A loose term for, "I am bigger than you, punk, therefore I will steal your piggybank."
2. What's mine is mine, what's yours is mine too
3. Distant cousin of Miscellaneous

Their retirement plan is written about as easy to understand as those Middle-English Chaucer poems. Not written in layman's terms makes it ambiguous, confusing and that's probably exactly how they intended it to be. Regardless, legislators have the nerve to pass a law that makes their own separate little retirement plan safe, warm, and cushiony, while ours is left out in the cold, starving and questionable for survival.

MORE FLEECING

One day, I was eating at an upscale restaurant. Deciding on an appetizer, I finally chose 'Fresh Roma Tomatoes in a Spicy, Jalapeno Relish with Tri-Colored Chips'. A few minutes later, the waiter puts down some water, bread, butter, chips and salsa. Ultimately, my entrée arrived. I told the waiter, "Excuse me, but I think you forgot the appetizer." He smiled and said, "No, it's right there" pointing to the chips and salsa. I paid $9.75 for chips and salsa? I am an idiot.

Well, in the world of Social Security:

1. The restaurant is our Legislators
2. I am the American public
3. The 'chips and salsa' is Social Security.

I allowed the restaurant to dupe my money into the Shakespearean-Described Chips and Salsa, like we are allowing our leaders to dupe taxpayer money into *their* Caesar-Brutus-Stab-You-In-The-Back retirement plan. Why didn't I go to the owner and object, "This is misleading, this is unethical." Just like, why aren't we going to the Legislators and saying the same thing—"This is misleading, this is unethical." They should not be privy to special retirement plans; they should be stuck in the huge Social Security mess with the rest of us.

Instead of 'Fresh Roma Tomatoes in a Spicy, Jalapeno Relish with Tri-Colored Chips', I wish America could order some "Fresh Senators and Congressmen Who Can Relish in the Tri-Characteristics of Ethics, Morals and Standards".

WHO SAID THIS?

"You will be guaranteed benefits as good as what members of Congress get."

... in a speech to the United Auto Workers in Washington, on March 22, 1994 [10]

Was it:

A. President George H.W. Bush
B. An unidentified member of Congress
C. Hillary Clinton
D. The President of General Motors

Actually, it was Hillary Clinton. She was the then, First Lady Hillary Rodham Clinton trying to push her healthcare plan to the public. She basically admitted that Congress has it good. And how convenient that six years later she would be privy to those same "good" "benefits".

*   *   *

The Capitol Building needs a welcome mat for
the doorway that says

ELITISTS NOT WELCOME

*   *   *

A VOICE MAIL, E-MAIL AND A MEMO

Technology Reflecting The Times

Voice Mail:

"Hi, this is Julie. Just calling to say hello and that I still haven't found a job. Call me back." I was going to call her back, but I had to run some errands first.

I was driving down the road and then realized my gas tank was low.Finding the nearest gas station, I *self-pumped* and *self-paid* my gas using my credit card, realizing I had no cash. Having no cash, I then drove to the nearest bank to got some money out of the *ATM Machine*. I was on my way to the local grocery store when I saw a sign on the door that said, "Out of Business". Sad that I could no longer shop at the grocery store I practically grew up in, I went to *Wal-Mart* and grabbed a few items. After going through the grocery store's *self check-out lane*, I realized I just shopped for the first time, without interacting with one human being.

I drove back to my apartment and grabbed my gate key to open the *automated gates* to my apartment complex. I knew the first thing I had to do was call Julie back, but I realized my electric bill was due. So I called the company to make a *payment-by-phone*. I know I could have *paid my bill online*, but my computer has been having so many problems lately! Remembering this, I dialed the computer online service center. It took a long time to get help because I was listening to the *automated instructions* of "Press 1 if this is in reference to your online account . . . press 2 if you wish to cancel or set-up a new account . . . press 3 if you are calling for technical problems. Ugh! I pressed 3 and ended up getting help from a representative named 'Joe' *located in India*. Finally, my errands were finished!

"Hi Julie, I got your message. I cannot figure out why you can't find a job".

E-Mail:

To: The Reader
From: Unknown Author
Subject: A Nation Divided

This is not an actual letter to Dear Abby, but rather—a humorous look at the ridiculous of our Republican-Democrat divided nation.

Dear Abby,

I am a crack dealer in Brooklyn who has recently been diagnosed as a carrier of Hepatitis. My parents live in a suburb of Eastbrooke and one of my sisters, who lives in the Bronx, is married to a transvestite.

My father and mother have recently been arrested for growing and selling marijuana. They are financially dependent on my other two sisters, who are prostitutes in New Jersey. I have two brothers. One is currently serving a non-parole life sentence for the murder of a teenage boy in 1994. My other brother is currently in jail awaiting trial on charges of sexual misconduct with his three children. I have recently become engaged to marry a former prostitute who lives in Alabama. She is still a part time "working girl". All things considered, I love my fiancé and look forward to bringing her into the family. I want to be totally open and honest with her.

This is my problem: Should I tell her about my cousin who is a Democrat?

Signed,
Worried About My Reputation

Memo:

To: President of the United States
From: A Taxpaying, Voting American
Subject: DEMUBLICANS

Message: Mr. President. I wonder how different our country would be if we had to chose from two candidates from the 'Demublican Party'. No special interests, no bi-partisan agendas, no mudslinging . . . just two candidates working toward the same goal. The goal of a steadfast and strong America.

*   *   *

"On account of being a democracy and run by the people, we are the only nation in the world that has to keep a government four years, no matter what it does."

—*Will Rogers (1879-1935)*[11]

CHAPTER 9

WITH LIBERTY

"The basis of a democratic state is liberty."

—*Aristotle (384 BC-322 BC) Politics[1]*

THE STATUE OF LIBERTY

She is the *Statue of Liberty* or *Lady Liberty*, but her formal title is *Liberty Enlightening the World*. Her home is the breathtaking island that welcomes visitors into New York Harbor. Today, it is known as Liberty Island, but it has changed names (and even hands) several times throughout history . . . here's the story.

In 1664, the English seized the island from the Mohegan Indians. The British sold it to Issack Bedloo, a New Amsterdam businessman, who named it Bedloe's Island. When he died in 1673, his daughter sold it to Adolphe Philipse and Henry Lane who used it as a quarantine station for New York City. In 1746, British Naval Commander Archibald Kennedy bought the island and changed the name to Kennedy Island. In 1759, New York State bought the island for 1,000 pounds. Sounds strange to have money in 'pounds' but keep in mind, it was not 'America' yet. New York State built a hospital on the island to help with quarantine efforts, for many immigrants were arriving in America with disease. The island changed purposes several times, everything from a French fleet station to a hospital.

The island even became property of the United States for defense purposes. [2]

In the end, New York and New Jersey signed a treaty deeding Bedloe's Island as New York jurisdiction and the docks and piers as New Jersey jurisdiction. That was in 1830 and the treaty still holds true today! The official name Liberty Island was bestowed on June 30, 1960.

Liberty Island is the Best 'Welcome Mat'
the U.S. Has to Offer!

And the Statue? We have France to thank for such a beautiful house-warming gift. Gustave Eiffel (Eiffel Tower, ring a bell?) was the structural engineer and Frederic Auguste Bartholdi was the sculptor. When Auguste Bartholdi visited America in 1871, he chose Bedloe'sIsland as his chosen spot to put his gigantic sculpture.

Construction for the Statue began in 1875 in France and was not completed until 1884. Back then, cargo was tough to "ship" (bad pun) so Lady Liberty was sent over in 214 crates filled with 350 individual pieces. In a separate project, another architect named Richard Morris Hunt created the granite pedestal in 1877.

The Statue was presented to America on July 4, 1884. President Grover Cleveland formally accepted the finalized gift at a ceremony on October 28, 1886. He stated: "We will not forget that liberty here made her home; nor shall her chosen altar be neglected".[3] And, neglected she wasn't. By September 1986, her construction costs reached $75 million. The Statue of Liberty was designated a National Monument on October 15, 1924.

*   *   *

"Smoking is one of the leading causes of statistics."

—Fletcher Knebel[4]

STATUE OF LIBERTY STATISTICS:[5]

Measurements

Height: 152 feet and 2 inches from the base to the torch

Weight: 450,000 pounds, which is 225 tons

(sorry Lady Liberty, I know a woman is never supposed to reveal her weight)

Symbols

Her Dress: a toga representing the Ancient Republic of Rome

Torch: represents Enlightenment

Chains Under Her Foot: represents Liberty crushing the chains of slavery

The Tablet: She holds it with her left hand and the inscription says "July 4, 1776" in Roman numerals, which is the date celebrating America's Independence from Britain.

7 Spikes In Her Crown Symbolize:
The Seven Seas: Arctic Ocean, Antarctic Ocean, North Atlantic Ocean, South Atlantic Ocean, North Pacific Ocean, South Pacific Ocean and the Indian Ocean

—or—

The Seven Continents: North America, South America, Europe, Asia, Africa, Antarctica and Australia

25 Windows In Her Crown: represent the 'natural minerals' of the earth

JUST HOW LARGE IS SHE?[6]

Length from heel to the top of her head: 111 feet, 1 inch

Length of her nose is 4 feet, 6 inches

There are 354 steps taking you up to the crown, which is 22 stories high

Her US women's shoe size based on a standard formula is 879 (wow! I'm a 7 ½)

4,000 square yards of approximate "fabric" used in Liberty's dress

*   *   *

THE STATUE OF LIBERTY SPEAKS FOR THE FIRST TIME
A Fundraising Poem Gives Her A Voice

In 1883, Emma Lazarus wrote a poem to help fundraising efforts for the Statue. Her words were engraved and placed on a bronze plaque at the base of the statue. This poem gives the illusion Lady Liberty is speaking.

The New Colossus

> Not like the brazen giant of Greek fame,
> With conquering limbs astride from land to land;
> Here at our sea-washed, sunset gates shall stand
> A mighty woman with a torch, whose flame
> Is the imprisoned lightning, and her name
> Mother of Exiles. From her beacon-hand
> Glows world-wide welcome; her mild eyes command

The air-bridged harbor that twin cities frame,
"Keep, ancient lands, your storied pomp!" cries she
With silent lips. "Give me your tired, your poor,
Your huddled masses yearning to breathe free,
The wretched refuse of your teeming shore,
Send these, the homeless, tempest-tost to me,
I lift my lamp beside the golden door!"

Emma Lazarus (1849-1887)[7]

* * *

**"Liberty means responsibility.
That is why most men dread it."**

—George Bernard Shaw 1856-1950[8]

Geez! She said, "Give me your tired, your poor" not "Give me your lazy, your unpatriotic". We are spoiled. Not too long ago, an election was held and the percentage of voter turnout was 18.2%. Not *eighty-one* percent, but *eight* percent! Can you imagine if those elections had not been held? There would have been riots and demonstrations in the streets, people screaming, "Let Us Vote! Let Us Vote!" Well, guess what America . . . men, women, citizens over age eighteen . . . most everyone can vote and what happens? No one shows up.

* * *

All human actions have one or more of these
seven causes: chance, nature, compulsion,
habit, reason, passion, and desire."

—Aristotle (384 BC—322 BC)[9]

1 MISTAKE, 2 MISTAKE, 3 MISTAKE, 4

> "Freedom is not worth having if it does not
> include the freedom to make mistakes."
>
> —*Mahatma Gandhi*[10]

In all this "Liberty" we have been showered with, it is often despoiled. Liberty comes with a price and often a mistake has to be paid for it. But, somehow there is a positive "silver-lining" in this dark cloud of mishaps, which enables our young country to learn from its' mistakes.

THE 2000 PRESIDENTIAL ELECTION:

Outcome—Despite having no idea what a hanging chad is, we realized . . . Yes, our vote *does* count!

THE MONICA LEWINSKY SCANDAL

Outcome—The harsh realization that our country takes tabloid news far more serious than hard news. And, being scandalous will get you an invite to Oscar parties

THE JANET JACKSON/JUSTIN TIMERLAKE HALFTIME SHOW AT SUPERBOWL 2004

Outcome-It took parents and kids in the same room watching the same show to finally realize that in the entertainment world *radicalism* is now *mainstream*

PRESIDENT BUSH'S IMMIGRATION LAW

Outcome—got INS officials off-the-hook when they were scratching their heads thinking,"How did so many get in here?"

SUDDEN INFILTRATION OF CABLE EDITORIAL NEWS SHOWS LIKE "HANNITY AND COLMES" "HARDBALL WITH CHRIS MATTHEWS" & "THE O'REILLY FACTOR"

Outcome—Even if you don't agree with what they think, at least they make you think.

DIXIE CHICKS BASHING OVERSEAS

Outcome-You can have the most beautiful singing voice in the world, but talk smack outside your own backyard and the neighbors will think your voice stinks.

JOHN KERRY IN THE SPOTLIGHT

Outcome-After decades of being ignored, Vietnam Veterans *finally* have a voice that is being heard . . . and that voice is stating they were unfairly and unjustly portrayed during the Vietnam Congressional Hearings in the early 1970's.

INTELLIGENCE FAILURES FROM THE WAR ON TERROR

Outcome—Realization that government agencies have a serious problem of "the right hand not knowing what the left hand is doing"

SEPTEMBER 11th

Outcome-America united and truly became one nation.

May we continue to learn and grow always finding a
silver-lining in our nation's cloud of liberty

*   *   *

HOLIDAY, AMERICAN-STYLE

The United States sure seems to have a ton of holidays! Actually, there are only ten federal holidays: New Year's Day, Martin Luther King Day, President's Day, Memorial Day, Independence Day, Labor Day, Columbus Day, Veterans Day, Thanksgiving Day and Christmas Day.

The word 'holiday' literally means 'holy day'. But, in America, 'holiday' has come to mean 'celebration'. Holidays vary in origin and meaning; some are religious, whereas others serve as a commemoration or festivity.

WHY DO THEY ALWAYS FALL ON A MONDAY?

The Uniforms Holiday Bill was signed by President Johnson on June 28, 1968, to insure a three-day weekend for Federal employees by celebrating four national holidays on Mondays—Washington's Birthday, Memorial Day, Veterans Day, and Columbus Day. The Uniforms Holiday Bill was created in an effort to help boost the economy. For if federal employees had four-day weekends, it was believed they would stimulate the economy through shopping and travel, for instance.

CALENDAR OF HOLIDAYS

Are you celebrating all the while having no idea *what* or *why* you are celebrating? Here's a little guideline.

Martin Luther King Jr. Holiday
3rd Monday in January

The idea for a commemorative holiday honoring Martin Luther King was first introduced in 1968, four days after King was assassinated. The legislation was introduced by

Congressman John Conyers (D) from Michigan. The bill was stalled, so a petition was created which had six million signatures! The petition was submitted to Congress and Representative Conyers and Representative Shirley Chisholm (D) of New York resubmitted the King legislation. Public coercion to pass the holiday mounted during the 1982 and 1983 civil rights marches in Washington. Congress finally passed the holiday legislation in 1983 and it was signed into effect by President Ronald Reagan.

Although King's birthday was on January 15th, a compromise moving the holiday from his birthday to the third Monday in January helped overcome opposition to the law because many felt the 15th was too close to the Christmas and New Year holidays. The third Monday in January was finally chosen as the official day honoring Martin Luther King, Jr.[11]

Groundhog Day
February 2nd

On February 2nd, clergy would bless candles and distribute them to the congregation. This was called Candlemas Day, a day observed for centuries throughout parts of Europe. Although Candlemas Day had a religious connotation, the tradition actually stemmed from the pagan celebration of Imbolc, the mid-point between the Winter Solstice and the Spring Equinox. It is believed that the ancient Romans brought the celebration of Imbolc to the Germans, where it ultimately spread throughout Europe. This old Scottish couplet echoes the ancient weather prediction from Candlemas Day that is associated with Groundhog Day today:

If Candlemas Day is bright and clear
There'll be two winters in the year

By the 1840s, Candlemas Day spread to the United States, particularly in parts of Pennsylvania whose earliest settlers were mostly German immigrants. The tradition evolved into the belief that if the groundhog sees its shadow on a "bright and clear" day, six more weeks of winter are ahead.

Punxsutawney, Pennsylvania is the birthplace of Groundhog Day, where the celebrated Groundhog "Punxsutawney Phil" looks for his shadow. The famous Gobbler's Knob, a mount just outside of Punxsutawney, is where this illustrious little groundhog makes his home.

The Star Power of Punxsutawney Phil—

During Prohibition—Phil threatened to impose 60 weeks of winter on the community if he wasn't allowed to drink.

1981—Phil wore a yellow ribbon paying homage to the American hostages in Iran.

1986—Phil met President Ronald Reagan along with Groundhog Club President Jim Means, Al Anthony and Bill Null.

1987—Phil met Pennsylvania Governor Dick Thornburg

1995—Phil made an appearance on the Oprah Winfrey Show! [12]

President's Day
Third Monday in February

February 12th and February 22nd honored the birthdays of Abraham Lincoln and George Washington, respectively. Both were celebrated individually, but eventually joined as a result of The Uniforms Holiday Bill. Remember The Uniforms Holiday Bill? It was the bill designed to insure three-day weekends for federal employees.

In 1971, President Richard Nixon proclaimed one single federal public holiday, Presidents' Day, to be observed on the 3rd Monday in February, and modified this holiday from not just honoring Lincoln and Washington, but all past presidents of the United States of America.

1. George Washington—1789-1797
2. John Adams—1797-1801
3. Thomas Jefferson—1801-1809
4. James Madison—1809-1817
5. James Monroe—1817-1825
6. John Quincy Adams—1825-1829
7. Andrew Jackson—1829-1837
8. Martin Van Buren—1837-1841
9. William Henry Harrison—1841
10. John Tyler—1841-1845
11. James Polk—1845-1849
12. Zachary Taylor—1849-1850
13. Millard Fillmore—1850-1853
14. Franklin Pierce—1853-1857
15. James Buchanan—1857-1861
16. Abraham Lincoln—1861-1865
17. Andrew Johnson—1865-1869
18. Ulysses S Grant—1869-1877
19. Rutherford B. Hayes—1877-1881
20. James A. Garfield—1881
21. Chester A. Arthur—1881-1885
22. S. Grover Cleveland—1885-1889
23. Benjamin Harrison—1889-1893
24. Grover Cleveland—1893-1897
25. William McKinley—1897-1901
26. Theodore (Teddy) Roosevelt—1901-1909
27. William Howard Taft—1909-1913
28. Woodrow Wilson—1913-1921
29. Warren G. Harding—1921-1923
30. Calvin Coolidge—1923-1929

31. Herbert Hoover—1929-1933
32. Franklin Delano Roosevelt—1933-1945
33. Harry S Truman—1945-1953
34. Dwight D. Eisenhower—1953-1961
35. John Fitzgerald Kennedy—1961-1963
36. Lyndon B. Johnson—1963-1969
37. Richard Nixon—1969-1974
38. Gerald Ford—1974-1977
39. James (Jimmy) Carter—1977-1981
40. Ronald Reagan—1981-1989
41. George Bush—1989-1993
42. William (Bill) Clinton—1993-2001
43. George W. Bush—2001[13]
44. Will U. Bepatriotic-1776—(I was just checking to see if you were really reading this list)

Whose In The Money?

$ 1-Bill—George Washington
$ 2-Bill—Thomas Jefferson
$ 5-Bill—Abraham Lincoln
$ 10-Bill—Alexander Hamilton
$ 20-Bill—Andrew Jackson
$ 50-Bill—Ulysses S. Grant
$100-Bill—Benjamin Franklin

No longer in print
$ 500-Bill—William McKinley
$ 1,000-Bill—Grover Cleveland
$ 5,000-Bill—James Madison
$ 10,000-Bill—Salmon P.Chase though not a president, he
   was the Secretary of the Treasury
$100,000-Bill—Woodrow Wilson

The law prohibits portraits of living persons from appearing on Government Securities. The designs were usually approved by the Secretary of the Treasury (aha! no wonder Salmon P. Chase made it onto the $10,000 bill), unless specified by an Act of Congress. The Commission On Fine Arts is responsible for approving all of the designs.

April Fool's Day
April 1st

There have been many festivals celebrating the concepts of foolery and trickery throughout history. One Roman festival in particular, The Saturnalia, involved a day of dancing, drinking, and merrymaking; where slaves pretended to rule their masters for the day.

It is unclear as to why this holiday falls on April 1, but this is one theory:

In 16th century Europe, New Years was celebrated on March 25th and the celebrations continued all the way through April 1st. In the mid-1560's, King Charles IX changed New Years Day from March 25th to January 1st to fall in sync with the Gregorian Calendar. Some people still celebrated New Years Day on April 1st instead of January 1st and those people were called April Fools. Each country has their own traditions in celebrating April Fool's Day. For example:

In France, the April Fool's is called "April Fish" (Poisson d'Avril). The French fool their friends by taping a paper fish to their friends' back and when some discovers this, they shout "Poisson d'Avril"!

In England, tricks can only be played in the morning hours and if a trick is successfully played on you, you are called a "noodle".

In Scotland, April Fools Day is 48 hours long and you are called an "April Gowk". A 'gowk' is another name for a cuckoo bird. April 2nd is called Taily Day and is dedicated to Pranks involving the rear-end. (you know, buttocks, booty . . . etc) The renown "Kick Me" sign placed on people's back was foremost in Scotland.[14]

In America, there are no rules. It is a fun and silly day to play practical jokes on just about everybody.

Mother's Day
2nd Sunday in May

This holiday is traced as far back as ancient Greece and Rome. Greeks celebrated a holiday in honor of Rhea, the mother of the gods. Romans celebrated a holiday in honor of Cybele, a mother goddess and the British Isles and Celtic Europe later celebrated the goddess Brigid, who was honored with a spring Mother's Day, linking the first milk of the ewes. Mothering Sunday was celebrated in Britain beginning around the 17th century, a day when apprentices and servants could return home for the day to visit their mothers. Unfortunately, by the 19th century, the holiday had almost completely died out.

The earliest Mothers' Day in America was initiated during 1858 in West Virginia. Anna Reeves Jarvis and Julia Ward Howe were the two women with the idea of promoting a "Mother's Day for Peace" to be celebrated on June 2. They tirelessly worked on peace efforts after the Civil War and Franco-Prussian War and Julia Ward Howe tried for years to establish a Mother's Day in America; but became better known as the author of the words to the "Battle Hymn of the Republic."

It was Anna Jarvis, the daughter of Anna Reeves Jarvis, who was the ultimate power behind the official establishment of Mother's Day. She swore at her mother's gravesite in 1905 that she would dedicate her life to her mother's project and establish a Mother's Day holiday. In 1907, she passed out 500 white carnations at St. Andrew's Methodist Episcopal Church in Grafton, West Virginia; her mother's church. Each mother in the congregation received a white carnation. On May 10 of the following year, at Anna Jarvis' request, that same church held a Sunday service honoring mothers.

The first bill was presented in the U.S. Senate proposing establishment of Mother's Day by Nebraska Senator Elmer Burkett. The proposal was not passed. Even though it was not an 'official' holiday, by 1909, Mother's Day services were unofficially being held in 46 states. Anna Jarvis quit her job and dedicated to working full-time writing letters to politicians, businessmen, clergy, and anyone else she thought might have some influence. It was when she enlisted the powerful World's Sunday School Association, a driving force in lobbying legislators and the U.S. Congress, that eventually helped to legislate this holiday. West Virginia became the first state to adopt an official Mother's Day in 1912 and in 1914, the U.S. Congress passed a Joint Resolution, signed by President Woodrow Wilson.

Something To Think About

Anna Jarvis became increasingly troubled over the commercialization of Mother's Day. She was quoted as saying, "I wanted it to be a day of sentiment, not profit.". She was against the revenue from selling flowers and called greeting cards "a poor excuse for the letter you are too lazy to write." [15] Did you know Mother's Day is believed to be the busiest day of the year for restaurants?

Memorial Day
Last Monday in May

It is a day to honor Americans who gave
their lives for their country

After the Civil War (1861-1865), many people in the North and South decorated graves of fallen soldiers with flowers. This day was originally called Decoration Day and was proclaimed on May 5, 1868 by General John Logan. Losing the Civil War was still fresh to the South, so they refused to acknowledge a holiday declared by Logan, a

Union officer. The South chose a separate day to honor their fallen soldiers. As a matter of fact, even to this day, most of the Southern States still have their own days for honoring their dead. For example, Mississippi holds the last Monday in April as Confederate Memorial Day and Texas declares Confederate Heroes Day on January 19.

In 1967, the name was changed to Memorial Day, honoring soldiers who had died, not just in the Civil War, but any war while serving the United States. Both North and South accepted Memorial Day and it was formally made a federal holiday by a law in 1971.

On Memorial Day, people place flowers and flags on the graves of military personnel. There are often times military parades and special programs, these programs often include the reading of Abraham Lincoln's "Gettysburg Address." Customarily, Memorials are dedicated on this day as well. That is why the World War II Memorial was dedicated in Washington D.C on Memorial Day 2004. Those who died at sea are honored as well. Several United States ports hold ceremonies where miniature ships filled with flowers are set afloat to sea.

Did you know?—in 1966, the U.S. government proclaimed Waterloo, New York, as the birthplace of this holiday. Citizens of Waterloo first observed Memorial Day on May 5, 1866, to honor soldiers killed in the Civil War. Businesses were closed, people decorated soldiers' graves and flew flags at half-mast, as a result, the traditional customs of Memorial day began.[16]

Father's Day
3rd Sunday in June

A woman named Sonora Smart Dodd thought of the idea of Father's Day when she was listening to a Mother's Day sermon in 1909 in Spokane, Washington. She was raised by her father, Henry Jackson Smart, after her mother died. Sonora adored her father. He was devoted and loving and she was grateful for all the sacrifices he had made raising her alone. She wanted her father to know how special he was to her. Since his birthday was in June, she chose to hold the first Father's Day celebration in Spokane, Washington on June, 19, 1910. In 1924, President Calvin Coolidge proclaimed the third Sunday in June as Father's Day.

The rose is the official Father's Day flower. The tradition is to wear a red rose in honor of a living father and a white rose if the father has died.[17]

p.s. Father's Day is the day there are more collect calls than any other day of the year.

This is the Operator. Will you accept a collect call from "Hi Dad! It's me, Joey! Happy Fath" Click. *Will you accept the charges, sir?*

**Flag Day
June 14**

On June 14, 1891, the Betsy Ross House in Philadelphia held a Flag Day celebration, honoring the anniversary of the Flag Resolution of 1777. On June 14 of the following year, the New York Society of the Sons of the Revolution, celebrated Flag Day again. Schools around the country began observing Flag Day with ceremonies and celebrations.

Flag Day was officially established by the Proclamation of President Woodrow Wilson on May 30th, 1916. While Flag Day was celebrated for years under Wilson's proclamation, it took over thirty years to make it an official holiday. On August 3rd, 1949, President Truman signed an Act of Congress designating June 14th of each year as National Flag Day.[18]

Independence Day
July 4

Independence Day, also called the Fourth of July, is the celebration of American colonies declaring the United States free and independent of Great Britain. Even though the Declaration of Independence was voted on and adopted July 2, 1776, it was sent to the printers who, upon completion, dated it July 4, 1776. John Hancock and Charles Thomson were the first to sign it on that day and most of the Delegates didn't sign it until August 2, 1776. To get an idea how slowly the news of America's independence traveled, Savannah, Georgia heard the news on August 10, 1776, while London, England finally heard about it on August 24, 1776.[19]

Labor Day
First Monday in September

Union Celebration, Chance For Votes or
Last Fling of Summer?

On the first Monday in September 1882, 10,000 members the Knights of Labor, took an unpaid day off and marched around Union Square in New York City in support of a holiday. This march was organized by Matthew Maguire, a New Jersey machinist and Peter J. McGuire, a New York carpenter. Being an election year, President Grover Cleveland seized the chance at appealing to these labor workers, for he wanted their vote. He therefore, enacted Labor Day as a national holiday.[20]

"Labor Day differs in every essential way from
the other holidays of the year in any country. All
other holidays are in a more or less degree
connected with conflicts and battles of man's

prowess over man, of strife and discord for greed
and power, of glories achieved by one nation over
another. Labor Day is devoted to no man, living
or dead, to no sect, race or nation."

Samuel Gompers
Founder and Longtime President of the Head of the
American Federation of Labor[21]

So, what do you think? Was Labor Day *really* established
as a Union protest, Union celebration, chance for votes or
the last federal holiday of summer?

LISA'S BIRTHDAY
September 25, 19(printer temporarily out of ink)

When people around the world rejoice and send gifts
to . . . just kidding

COLUMBUS DAY
Second Monday in October

In 1792, a ceremony was organized by the Society of
St. Tammany, or the Colombian Order of New York City.
The ceremony honored Christopher Columbus and the
300th anniversary of his landing in America. Out of pride
for their fellow Italian, the Italian population of New
York organized the first celebration of the discovery of
America on October 12, 1866. It was not called Columbus
Day until 1869 when Italians in San Francisco gave it
that name. Colorado became the first state to observe a
Columbus Day in 1905 and since 1920, Columbus Day has
been celebrated annually. In 1937, under President Franklin
Roosevelt, every October 12th was proclaimed Columbus
Day. It became a federal public holiday under President
Johnson in 1968.[22]

p.s. Historically, Christopher Columbus was not the first to discover America nor the first European to land in America. The myth that Christopher Columbus 'discovered' America was fueled by Washington Irving's biography of Columbus, which exaggerated the truth of his voyages.

Halloween
October 31st

Throughout Europe, November 1st was All Saints' Day (All Hallow's Day) in the Roman Catholic and Anglican churches. The night before, October 31st, was known as All Hallow's Eve. In preparation for All Saint's Day on November 1st, evil spirits had to be scared off, and as a result, jack-o-lanterns and other Halloween customs were popularized.

Immigrants from Great Britain and Ireland brought the Halloween tradition to the U.S., but the holiday itself was not popular in America. It wasn't until the latter part of the 19th century, when Irish immigrants arrived in large masses after The Potato Famine of 1840, that the popularity of the holiday returned and has since remained popular today.[23]

Veteran's Day
November 11

World War I ended the 11th month, the 11th day, on the 11th hour. In an Act approved May 13, 1938, the 11th of November became a holiday known as 'Armistice Day.' After World War II and the Korean War, Congress amended the Act of 1938 by striking out the word "Armistice" and inserting the word "Veterans". On June 1, 1954, November 11th was the day chosen to honor American veterans of all wars.

The first Veterans Day under the new law was observed with much confusion on October 25, 1971. President Gerald R. Ford realized the significance of this holiday to many Americans, so on September 20, 1975, he signed into Public Law which returned the annual observance of Veterans Day to its original date of November 11, which went into effect in 1978.[24]

*   *   *

BACK TO MARTIN LUTHER KING JR

"They that can give up essential liberty to obtain
a little temporary safety deserve neither liberty
nor safety."

Benjamin Franklin (1706-1790)
Historical Review of Pennsylvania, 1759[25]

Benjamin Franklin's words seem to predict the safety Martin Luther King Jr. sacrificed in attaining civil liberty. Though he is known mostly for his monumental "I Have A Dream" speech, I was ashamed to not know that much about Martin Luther King, Jr. To have his own holiday, I knew there had to be something special about him. After looking into his life, it is evident that yes, this charismatic and eloquent speaker was indeed, very special.

Dr. Martin Luther King, Jr. was born in Atlanta, Georgia. He graduated from Morehouse College with a Bachelor of Arts in 1948 and Crozer Theological Seminary with a B.D. in 1951. He received his Ph.D from Boston University in 1955. He became a minister of a Baptist church in Montgomery, Alabama, gaining prestige as a civil-rights leader after leading a black boycott of segregated city bus lines during 1955 and in 1956. When Montgomery buses began to operate on a desegregated basis, Martin Luther King Jr. gained critical acclaim for his peaceful methods of demonstrating and using nonviolent means of lifting racial oppression.[26]

King organized the Southern Christian Leadership Conference (SCLC). This organization was started in the South and eventually spread nationwide. His philosophy of nonviolent resistance led to numerous arrests throughout the 1950s and 60s. He received international attention with a protest in Birmingham, Alabama in 1963. In August of that same year, he led the March on Washington, participated by over 200,000 people.

In 1964, he was awarded the Nobel Peace Prize. King graciously accepted the award by stating it as "an award for the world civil rights movement and its dedicated leaders" encouraging it to "inspire all of us to work a little harder and with more determination to make the American Dream a reality."[27]

Sadly, on April 4, 1986 he was shot and killed as he stood on the balcony of the Lorraine Motel in Memphis, Tennessee. He was in Memphis to support a strike by the city's sanitation workers. The Lorraine Motel has since become a civil-rights museum. He was only thirty-nine years old when he died, leaving a wife and four young children. Dr. Martin Luther King's widow, Coretta Scott King, graciously continued his civil rights mission[28.]

.

*   *   *

"If physical death is the price that I must pay to free my white brothers and sisters from a permanent death of the spirit, then nothing can be more redemptive."

Martin Luther King, Jr.
On learning of threats on his life, June 5, 1964[29]

* * *

Martin Luther King Jr.'s famous speech embodied the spirit and essence of the Civil Rights movement. Notice in the following excerpt, King cleverly coupled the concept of 'civil liberty' with 'cashing a check'. It was delivered on the steps at the Lincoln Memorial in Washington D.C. on August 28, 1963.

Excerpts from "I Have A Dream" by Martin Luther King, Jr.[30]

Five score years ago, a great American, in whose symbolic shadow we stand signed the Emancipation Proclamation. This momentous decree came as a great beacon light of hope to millions of Negro slaves who had been seared in the flames of withering injustice. It came as a joyous daybreak to end the long night of captivity. But one hundred years later, we must face the tragic fact that the Negro is still not free. One hundred years later, the life of the Negro is still sadly crippled by the manacles of segregation and the chains of discrimination. One hundred years later, the Negro lives on a lonely island of poverty in the midst of a vast ocean of material prosperity. One hundred years later, the Negro is still languishing in the corners of American society and finds himself an exile in his own land.

So we have come here today to dramatize an appalling condition. In a sense we have come to our nation's capital to cash a check. When the architects of our republic wrote the magnificent words of the Constitution and the Declaration of Independence, they were signing a promissory note to which every American was to fall heir. This note was a promise that all men would be guaranteed the inalienable rights of life, liberty, and the pursuit of happiness. It is obvious today that America has defaulted on this promissory note insofar as her citizens of color are concerned. Instead of honoring this sacred obligation, America has given the Negro people a bad check which has come back marked "insufficient funds." But we refuse to believe that the bank of justice is bankrupt. We refuse to believe that there are insufficient funds in the great vaults of opportunity of this nation.

So we have come to cash this check—a check that will give us upon demand the riches of freedom and the security of justice. We have also come to this hallowed spot to remind America of the fierce urgency of now.

. . . . I still have a dream. It is a dream deeply rooted in the American dream. I have a dream that one day this nation will rise up and live out the true meaning of its creed:

"We are not makers of history.
We are made by history."

—Martin Luther King Jr.[31]

MORE RACIAL OBSTACLES

In March of 2004, racial equality was challenged again, this time, in defense of Caucasians. It happened at Roger Williams University in Rhode Island. A student named Jason Mattera of Brooklyn, New York stated, "This is what college is all about, challenging the status quo"[32] and created a $250 Whites-Only Scholarship. He asked applicants to write an essay on "Why you are proud of your White heritage"- a takeoff on other minority scholarships that ask similar "Why you are proud of your Hispanic heritage" or "What your Black heritage means to you".

Ironically, Mattera is originally from Puerto Rico and went to college on scholarship from the Hispanic College Fund. Therefore, the scholarship was not a personal schema, but rather a parody on minority scholarships. The scholarship was publicly criticized by Ed Gillespie, Chairman of the Republican National Committee. Because Mattera had previously founded the Roger Williams University College Republicans, Gillespie stated in a

February 17th letter to Madera that the scholarship conveys a "message of exclusion".[33]

Is Gillespie kidding? And the "Why you are proud of your Hispanic heritage" does not? The original intention of Affirmative Action was supposed to be to remedy discrimination against racial and ethnic minorities and women. But all it has done is dictate racial quotas to the extent of segregation, which is the exact opposite of the original intention of Affirmative Action in the first place!

The hypocrisy of Affirmative Action brings me back to the idea of . . . Asian/American, Irish/American, Mexican/American . . . can't we all just say American?

*   *   *

"People will accept your ideas much more readily
if you tell them Benjamin Franklin said it first."

—*David H. Comins*[34]

CHAPTER 10

AND JUSTICE FOR ALL

*"A hero is no braver than an ordinary man, but he is
braver five minutes longer."*

—*Ralph Waldo Emerson (1803-1882)* [1]

* * *

And Justice for all . . . and Jordan for all . . . and Evert-
Lloyd for all . . . and O'Neal for all . . . and Woods for all . . .

People put professional athletes up on pedestals. I was
no different, I admit it. I cut my hair like Dorothy Hamill
and ran around the tennis court planning on being the next
Chris Evert-Lloyd. I was especially mesmerized by the Coca-
Cola commercial where Mean Joe Green tossed his shirt to
the little boy and the kid looked up and said, "Wow! Thanks
Mean Joe!" I remember feeling that I too would one day
meet my hero, therefore drinking Coca-Cola was imperative
in my upbringing. I knew one day my hero would walk up
to me and have a sip of MY drink. It never happened. I was
so disappointed and have been disillusioned with heroes
ever since.

As a little girl, I was surrounded by surreal models for
heroes. Turn on the television and there was Superman
saving Lois Lane. Change the channel and there was Peggy
Fleming winning the Olympic gold medal. The word *hero*
seemed to be everywhere. Poor ole' Peanut-Butter and Jelly

Sandwich. It was alright, but if you wanted a really, really big sandwich you had to order a Hero Sandwich. It seemed every movie ended with the bad guy losing and the good guy holding a girl swooning "You're my hero!"

Then the word *hero* wasn't strong enough anymore. Not to outdo the "Hero" title Superman earned, Wonder Woman, Batman and others joined the elite group of "Superheroes".

Soon we'll have "Mega-Superheroes"

Then, "Ultra-Mega Superheroes"

Once again I must go back to the concept of Cola.

Remember good-old *Cola*?

Then, we were introduced to *Diet Cola*

Then, *Caffeine-Free Cola*

Then, *Diet Caffeine-Free Cola*

Soon we'll have **Caffeine-Free Ultra Diet Cola Superheroes**

We Americans, enough is never enough.

How strange that a person who gets to play basketball for a living, something most of us do for pleasure, can earn in the millions of dollars. Yet, a teacher, someone who spends over forty-hours a week exhaustingly teaching the youth of America, earns around twenty-four thousand a year. Professional athletes do not put their life on the line to play a sport, yet they are adored and worshipped by millions of people. However, a policeman or a fireman, someone who risks their life not for themselves, but for you, is earning roughly the same amount as that teacher. It's the teachers, policeman, fireman and soldiers we *should* worship . . . but are too fascinated with the romance and glamour portrayed by professional sports.

> **"For a list of all the ways technology has failed to improve the quality of life, please press three."**
>
> —*Alice Kahn*[2]

The problem is, we are an instantaneous society. If you need money, go to the ATM.If you need a movie, order Pay-Per-View. If you need to shop, turn on the Home Shopping Network. If you need fast-food, go to . . . stop! What restaurant comes to mind? McDonald's, right? Aha! Even you the reader has already put McDonald's into the category "hero of the fast-food chain". What about Taco Bell? What about Burger King? Society has a preconceived notion as to what "the top" should be.

This same concept also applies to our heroes. We demand instant gratification from them. Just like not wanting to wait patiently for a hamburger, we demand a *higher* world-record . . . a *higher* jackpot . . . a *higher* multi-million dollar contract . . .

WHO WAS THE FIRST HERO?

The word 'hero' is likely derived from the ancient Egyptian genius 'Heron of Alexandria.' In 62 A.D, Heron lived in Alexandria, Egypt and recorded several works in the areas of mathematics, physics and mechanics. His knowledge in several subjects was unprecedented, though his greatest claim to fame was his depiction of the first steam-powered engine.

HERO OR HERO WORSHIP?

These two definitions from the Merriam-Webster Online Dictionary explain the difference between *hero* and *hero worship*.[3]

Hero
Main Entry: he·ro
Pronunciation: 'hir-(")O, 'hE-(")rO
Function: noun

Etymology: Latin heros, from Greek hErOs
Date: 14th century
1 a : a mythological or legendary figure often of divine descent endowed with great strength or ability b : an illustrious warrior c : a man admired for his achievements and noble qualities d : one that shows great courage . . .
4 : an object of extreme admiration and devotion : IDOL

Hero Worship
Main Entry: hero worship
Function: noun
Date: 1774
1 : veneration of a hero
2 : foolish or excessive adulation for an individual

It is evident America is a society of hero worship, not heroes.

YOU ARE NOW MY "MIRUS"

Our society should just erase the entire notion of *hero* and *hero worship* and instead, model after the Greek word mirus. Mirus is to admire in a way as to version your life comparable to whom you admire, but at the same time, be successful in your own right. Our kids should not be saying, "I want to be like Shaquille O'Neal." Our kids should say, "I want to excel in basketball to the point where I can compete against Shaquille O'Neal—and win!" If we could achieve that . . . then we would not worship heroes, we would become them.

Today, as an adult, I don't know who to hero worship anymore. But you know, the funny thing is, growing up it seemed everyone in the world was a hero, except my parents. They were strict and made me go to school and clean my room. Yuck.How ironic that today I live in a world where no one is my hero . . . *except my parents.*

OUR COUNTRY'S MOST CHERISHED HEROES

The Congressional Medal of Honor is the highest honor bestowed upon any American. It is given to military personnel who demonstrate extraordinary valor during a time of crisis. It was originally established during the Civil War to promote and recognize competence in the Navy, but today, is granted to any section of the armed forces. Out of over 40 million American men and women who have served in our armed forces, roughly 3,500 have received this most coveted honor. Approximately 130 of them are alive today. These people are said to have "received" never "won" the Congressional Medal of Honor, which is presented by the President of the United States in the name of Congress.

HEROES ON HORSES

Did you know . . . if a statue in the park of a person on a horse has both front legs in the air, the person died in battle. If the horse has one front leg in the air, the person died as a result of wounds received in battle. If the horse has all four legs on the ground, the person died of natural causes.

p.s. if the horse poops, it's not a statue.

*   *   *

A man dies and goes to Heaven. St. Peter is standing at the Pearly Gates, holding the keys to Heaven and says to the man, "Before I let you in, I must hear of a good deed you did in your life."

"Well, I can think of one thing," the man offers. "Once, on a trip to Brooklyn, I came upon a gang of dangerous hoodlums on motorcycles who were threatening a young woman. I stood up to the entire group of thugs. I told them to leave her alone, but they wouldn't listen. So I approached the largest, meanest and most heavily tattooed biker. I kicked his motorcycle over, punched him in the face, ripped out his nose ring and threw it on the ground. I told him, 'Leave her alone or you'll have to deal with me!"

St. Peter was so impressed. "When did this happen?"

"Just a couple of minutes ago."

*   *   *

Everyone is necessarily the hero of his own life story.

—*John Barth (1930-)*[4]

How ironic that in our quest to find heroes, we look everywhere but inside ourselves, as this poem suggests.

A Hero in the Mirror

David and Goliath and Romeo and Juliet
Immortalized stars whose bravery set a precedent
The heroes of old with such courage and command
Never afraid to die or to make a stand

The breathtaking tales of the champions of old
Always a knight in shining armor to behold
But in this modern world so doubtful and unsure
Heroes, like legends, are mere stories of literature

Here in the mirror as I gaze to see
Who is this stranger looking back at me?
Not a Nobel Prize winner or a 'toast of the town'
This image is of failure, no recognition to be found

I reflect further, not in the mirror, this time in my soul
There I find what mythological legends never disclose
The soul reveals not through materialism is heroism achieved
But a deeper success that one cannot see

The soul is a hero whose word and handshake are true
Finding happiness in family, friends, family friends, old and
    new
A soul grateful for life's blessings at the will of God's pace
And handling tragedy with both resolute and grace

Though Heron of Alexandria may be the first hero known
    to man
I wonder if he ever found his hero within his own spirit?
You will search all your life for a hero, it's true
And the most significant is the one ultimately found in you.

*   *   *

"We can't all be heroes because somebody has to
sit on the curb and clap as they go by."

—*Will Rogers (1879-1935)*[5]

MY HERO

My hero is incredibly brave. She traveled across the
Atlantic Ocean completely alone, having no idea what was
in store for her. She traveled in search for a way of life that
would give her the liberty she longed for. She suffered
through war and witnessed the loss of countless lives.
Indeed, war came with a price. But finally, the goal of
democracy was achieved.

She was respected, beloved and cherished. People were
captivated by her. She broadened horizons, while warmly
embracing any guest who came to stay. As years passed, she
longed for others throughout the world to feel the splendor of
freedom she so enjoyed. Once again, many lives were lost at
war, but she was determined to let the world experience the
beauty of having 'life, liberty and the pursuit of happiness'.

As years passed, domestic hostility around her was
intensifying. People she believed to be her avid supporters

were suddenly in conflict over everything from the Civil War to Civil Rights; from political partisanship to political partition; from disagreement to dissention. She became very sad. This was not the reason she risked everything to come to this new land. She had gone through too much to have her establishment questioned. How could her people be in discord when they have something so rare and beautiful? Democracy is an extraordinary achievement! Full of pride, she wanted everyone to rejoice, not clash, in the success of her triumph!

Today, though aged, she still stands with great strength. As she prevails, it is important to her that everyone recognize the sacrifice she made in her determination to be free. Her final wish is that we protect this wonderful tradition with all our might. Never treacherous. Never apathetic. Never forget and always appreciate, how incredibly blessed we are.

My hero has a name. Her name is America.

THE GREAT AMERICAN CHALLENGE:

A motto of the United States is "E Pluribus Unum" meaning, *Out of Many, One.* Indeed, this is the basis of our country. Out of many, we are one. One individual granted a precious gift. It is our civic duty that as this 'one', we must assimilate into a unified 'many'.

Politicians:	*Get rid of personal political agendas and work together*
Media:	*Report intelligently and responsibly*
Celebrities:	*Be accountable for your high-profile status (which you chose)*
Anti-War Demonstrators:	*Respect the men and women in the military who think you merit fighting and dying for*
Military:	*Present a good image overseas and continue making us proud here at home*

Naturalized Citizens: *Love your birth country and cherish its culture, but respect the new country by which you have chosen allegiance*

America's Kids: *Learn about America's past and envision where you can be a part of America's future*

America's Adults: *Improve both the State of the Union and the State of Your Personal Union with the United States.*

Every American: Have "*That Look*"

LOW-CARB PATRIOTS

The survival of our democracy is dependent on us, the 'Low-Carb Patriots'-the patriots of the twenty-first century. In a quest to understand this nation divided, we spent the last ten chapters sweating out this American diet of patriotism, facts, history and pop-culture, yet, do you suppose all we Low-Carb Patriots really need is . . . a little sugar?

Perhaps this "sugar" is found in the words of Warren Harding, when he expressed the needs of America back in 1920.

"America's present need is not heroics, but healing; not nostrums but normalcy; not revolution, but restoration."

Warren G. Harding (1865-1923)
Speech in Boston in 1920[6]

COOL DOWN

. . . pause now and take a deep breath . . . contemplate the beauty of the freedom that has been bestowed upon you. Many countries experience oppression, dictatorship and suffering; many will never know the splendor of living as we do.

*   *   *

FINAL CHALLENGE

"Nearly all men can stand adversity, but if you
want to test a man's character, give him power."

—*Abraham Lincoln (1809-1865)*[7]

Heroes are everywhere . . . wonderful and amazing
people, who inspire, encourage and motivate us. A hero
does not have to be glamorous or awe-inspiring, just
someone who has in some way made a difference.
Unfortunately, we never let them know the significant
impact they made on our life.

Now, here's your chance.

Give this last page to someone who is a hero to you . . .

FOR YOU, MY HERO

"You will search all your life for a hero, it's true
And the most significant is the one ultimately
found in you."

-*Lisa Malooly*

"Perhaps, after all, America never has been discovered. I myself would say that it had merely been detected."

Oscar Wilde (1854-1900)[8]

THE END

ENDNOTES

TABLE OF CONTENTS

1   http://www.quotationspage.com

CHAPTER 1 I Pledge Allegiance

1   http://www.quotationspage.com
2   Ibid
3   Ibid
4   Ibid
5   Ibid
6   Ibid
7   Ibid
8   U.S. Embassy to Germany http://www.usembassy.de/usa/ etexts/speeches/pres/3.htm
9   U.S. Embassy to Germany http://www.usembassy.de/usa/ etexts/gov/bushinaug.htm
10   http://www.quotationspage.com
11   U.S. Embassy to Germany http://www.usembassy.de/usa/ etexts/his/e_factpostwar.htm
12   http://bensguide.gpo.gov/3-5/state/dc.html
13   Ibid
14   http://bensguide.gpo.gov/3-5/symbols/eagle.html
15   http://bensguide.gpo.gov/3-5/symbols/rose.html
16   http://www.thexaminer.org/volume6/number6/empire.htm
17   http://www.quotationspage.com

CHAPTER 2 To The Flag

1   U.S. Embassy to Germany http://www.usembassy.org.uk/rcflags.html
2   Ibid
3   U.S. Embassy to Germany http://www.usembassy.org.uk/rcflags.html
4   Ibid
5   U.S. Embassy to Germany http://www.usembassy.org.uk/rcflags.html
6   Ibid
7   http://www.ushistory.org/betsy/flaglife.html
8   Ibid
9   Ibid
10   http://www.ushistory.org/key/flaglife.html
11   Ibid
12   Ibid
13   Ibid
14   Ibid
15   Ibid
16   http://www.quotationspage.com
17   http://www.mville.edu/athletics/sports/wbask/02_03_season_roster/Toni_Smith.htm
18   http://www.quotationspage.com
19   Ibid

CHAPTER 3 Of the United States of America

1   http://www.quotationspage.com
2   http://www.census.gov/populations/socdemo/ancestry/table_05.txt
3   http://www.census.gov/populations/socdemo/ancestry/table 05.txt Internet release date February 18, 1998
4   Bureau of the Census and Bureau of Economic Analysis press release: U.S. International Trade in Goods and Services: March 2004.
5   http://www.quotationspage.com Quotations from Lichty and Wagner, Twain, Menchen, Hugo, Rogers and Thompson

6   http://www.ourdocuments.gov/doc.php?flash=false&
     doc=23
7   Ibid.
8   http://www.terrorismanswers.com/policy/foreignaid2.html
9   http://www.globalissues.org/TradeRelated/Debt/
     USAid.asp
10   http://www.terrorismanswers.com/policy/foreignaid2.html
11   Ibid
12   Ibid
13   http://www.globalissues.org/TradeRelated/Debt/
     USAid.asp
14   http://www.terrorismanswers.com/policy/foreignaid2.html
15   Ibid.
16   http://usinfo.state.gov/mena/Archive_Index/
     The_Camp_David_Accords.html
17   Firstgov Your First Click To The U.S. Government http://
     www.whitehouse.gov/whmo/camp-david.html
18   http://www.quotationspage.com

CHAPTER 4 And To The Republic

1   http://www.quotationspage.com
2   Ibid.
3   Ibid.
4   Ibid.
5   Ibid.
6   Ibid.
7   Ibid.
8   Reprinted by permission of Forbes Magazine c 2004 Forbes
     Inc.
9   Ibid.
10   http://www.quotationspage.com.
11   Ibid.
12   Reprinted with permission by the Associated Press
13   Reprinted with permission by the Associated Press
14   http://www.quotationspage.com

CHAPTER 5 For Which It Stands

1   http://www.quotationspage.com
2   http://www.mediaresearch.org/cyberalerts/2003/ cyb20030429.asp#4
3   Ibid.
4   Ibid.
5   http://www.quotationspage.com
6   Ibid.
7   Ibid.
8   U.S. Embassy to Germany http://www.usembassy.de/usa/ government-seal.htm
9   http://www.quotationspage.com
10 U.S. Embassy to Germany http://www.us embassy.de/ search/index.html "Biographies of Cabinet Members" (political resumes)
11 www.allmovieportal.com (celebrity resumes)
12 http://www.quotationspage.com
13 http://www.quotationspage.com
14 www.lastarz.com
15 http://www.quotationspage.com
16 Ibid.

CHAPTER 6 One Nation

1   http://www.quotationspage.com
2   Ibid.
3   Ibid.
4   http://www.wordorigins.org/
5   Ibid.
6   Ibid.
7   Ibid.
8   Ibid.
9   Ibid.
10 Ibid.
11 Ibid.

12 Ibid.
13 http://www.cia.gov/cia/publications/factbook *The World Factbook*
14 Ibid.
15 http://www.quotationspage.com
16 Ibid.
17 author unknown

CHAPTER 7 Under God

1   http://www.quotationspage.com
2   www.governmentguide.com
3   Ibid
4   http://www.quotationspage.com
5   http://www.aclu.org/aboutr/aboutmain.cfm
6   http://www.cia.gov/cia/publications/factbook/geos/xx.htm *The World Factbook*
7   http://www.quotationspage.com
8   http://www.plato.stanford.edu/entries/actualism/possibilism.html
9   http://www.quotationspage.com
10 Ibid
11 U.S. Embassy to Germany http://www.usembassy.de/usa/government.seal-print.htm
12 Ibid
13 http://www.quotationspage.com

CHAPTER 8 Indivisible

1   http://www.quotationspage.com
2   Ibid.
3   http://www.armscontrolcenter.org/terrorism/101/timeline.html
4   http://www.quotationspage.com
5   http://www.freerepublic.com/focus/f-news/1028727/posts
6   http://www.quotationspage.com

7 http://bensguide.gpo.gov/3-5/symbols/americathe beautiful.html
8 Ibid.
9 http://www.quotationspage.com
10 http://www.rpc.senate.gov/-rpc/releases/1998/tsp-jt.htm
11 http://www.quotationspage.com

CHAPTER 9 With Liberty

1 http://www.quotationspage.com
2 http://www.endex.com/gf/buildings/liberty/libertyfacts.htm
3 Ibid.
4 http://www.quotationspage.com
5 www.endex.com/gf/buildings/liberty/libertyfacts.htm
6 Ibid.
7 Ibid.
8 http://www.quotationspage.com
9 Ibid.
10 Ibid.
11 U.S. Embassy to Germany http://www.usembassy.de/usa/holidays-mlking.htm
12 www.groundhog.org/
13 U.S. Embassy to Germany http://www.usembassy.de/usa/holidays-
14 U.S. Embassy to Germany http://www.usembassy.de/usa/holidays-
15 Reprinted with permission. Copyright 2004* Louie Volpe Holidays on the Net—*www.holidays.net*
16 U.S. Embassy to Germany http://www.usembassy.de/usa/holidays-memorial.htm
17 U.S. Embassy to Germany http://www.usembassy.de/usa/etexts/hol/celbrate.pdf.htm
18 U.S. Embassy to Germany http://www.usembassy.de/usa/holidays-fun.htm
19 U.S. Embassy to Germany http://www.usembassy.de/usa/holidays-fourth.htm

20 U.S. Embassy to Germany http://www.usembassy.de/usa/etexts/hol/laborday.htm

21 Ibid.

22 U.S. Embassy to Germany http://www.usembassy.de/usa/holidays-columbus.htm

23 U.S. Embassy to Germany http://www.usembassy.de/usa/holidays-halloween.htm

24 U.S. Embassy to Germany http://www.usembassy.de/usa/holidays-veterans.htm

25 http://www.quotationspage.com

26 http://memory.loc.gov/ammem/today/jan15.html

27 Ibid.

28 Ibid.

29 http://www.quotationspage.com

30 http://www.usconstitution.net/dream.html

31 http://www.quotationspage.com

32 Reprinted with the permission of the Associated Press

33 Reprinted with the permission of the Associated Press

34 http://www.quotationspage.com

CHAPTER 10 And Justice For All

1 http://www.quotationspage.com

2 Ibid.

3 By permission. From Merriam-Webster Online Dictionary c 2004 by Merriam-Webster, Incorporated (www.Merriam-Webster.com)

4 http://www.quotationspage.com

5 Ibid.

6 Ibid.

7 Ibid.

8 Ibid

Thank-you to two amazing patriots and friends, Steve and Carol Sasfy for your input and suggestions. Also, to my dearest friend DeDe Robbins, a lifelong friend since the first grade, always loyal and always encouraging.

A special thank-you to Anup Shah for your kindness and fabulous website

A special thank-you to Gary Feuerstein, whose dedication to Lady Liberty is so incredibly admirable

A special thank-you to Dave Wilton, who knows more about English than this old lady

English teacher—I can't wait to read your book

A special thank-you to Linda Mirabella-what a neat person you are!

A special thank you to graphic artist Natascha Cozby.

Heartfelt thanks Joe Raganas at Xlibris for your talent and vision. Everyone at Xlibris, thank you.

A final thank-you to Glen Holbrook Photography for the photo in the back